Love Notes

a biblical look at love

Ryan Dalgliesh

EDITED BY CAITLIN JORDAN

xulon
PRESS

Love Notes
a biblical look at love
by Ryan Dalgliesh

Printed in the United States of America

ISBN 978-1-60477-687-4

www.xulonpress.com

TABLE OF CONTENTS:

DEDICATION:

11-10-97

My beloved wife,

It is 12:45 a.m. and because I do not feel well, I have been unsuccessful in finding any sleep. It is now with great excitement that I write these words. You see, beautiful, this is the beginning of my notes on love. You are ever on my mind, so it is only natural I type this thinking of you. I cannot help but wonder if I have met you already; but know that I love you. If these notes ever become successful—or if they merely stay a private file—they are dedicated to you and to God who has taught me how to love you already. Though I have previously written notes in a spiral notebook, this is my first attempt at a love workbook. I am praying for you as I write this. I love you.

Always,
ryan

To my beautiful wife wherever you are
tonight; my dear sister and faithful friend,
my encourager, may you ever say of me that
I have loved you rightly.

1-20-08

I would like to dedicate this book to my now wife, Michele. These pages reflect years of waiting and praying for you. I started the process of studying this that I might know how to love you well. Who knew it would take ten years for God to bring you into my life. You are a treasure and a joy to me every day. I love you so much! Thanks for being gracious and compassionate. Thanks for making me laugh from the very first time that we spoke. Thanks for loving God and His word. I look forward to many more years of loving you and being loved by you.

CHAPTER ONE

THINGS YOU SHOULD KNOW

It is with great trepidation that I write this. I mean, come on, who am I that I should tell you what the Bible has to say about love? Still, that is why I am writing this, and to learn about love must be why you are reading it. In the following pages I will do my best to impart to you everything that God has taught me on love. Please understand my knowledge is not complete and my wisdom is not deep, but I am confident everything I tell you God has given me. My prayer is that, as I work this in to some sort of organized form and as you partake in the reading and studying of my notes, we both will grow. I believe we have gotten so far away from what love is that most of us are uncertain as to what it is supposed to look like. If this book can be a tool by which you come to understand overall love a little better—and later romantic love—then Praise Be to God!

ryan

3-8-99

It has been sixteen months since I first sat down to write these notes; they had been floating around in my head up until that point. Now as I teach these notes on Sunday mornings to a group of college students and as I begin to rewrite, reword, or just plain remove some of my previous words, several things strike me. One, time goes by way too fast. Two, for someone with an understanding of what Biblical love looks like, I sure do not do such a great job of living it. Finally, as I sit here writing, I can't help wondering, how does God love me? Why does God even care? Why would He spend time on me? You see, right now I'm feeling unlovely; it seems sometimes even though I know all the right answers, I just can't bring myself to understand God's love for me. Sure I teach about God's love and can show you time and time again in the Scripture what God's love looks like and how He intended it for me, but somehow today I just feel as though no one could love me. Sometimes feelings of unloveliness stem from the feeling that I do not measure up to expectations held of me. Sometimes it has to do with the overwhelming stench of my sin. And sometimes it just has to do with me not liking myself on a given day. "If I don't even like me, how can God?" A ridiculous question I know, but it has plagued me before.

I am certain many of you have felt, and do feel, the same way. Some of you perhaps have tears welling up in your eyes because you feel so unlovely. So now I write for all to read that which I have taught scores of times; I do so that it may benefit you as you read and me as I write.

3-12-01
To you the reader,

It is amazing how time can change things. If you had asked me when I began this study on Biblical love back in August 1996, or even when I first put it to paper in November 1997, why I did it—why I pursued an understanding of Love from the stand-point of the bible—I would have had to answer something in regard to a future wife. If you will look at the first paragraph you will take note my heart was set heavily upon my future spouse. Now, years later, I sit late at night at the computer working again on this great study that has been a large part of my maturing years in the Christian faith, and my thoughts turn to you, the reader. My desire for a wife seems to fade more and more, but I will not go into it in great detail now. Over the last few years I have taught these notes to hundreds, and maybe thousands, of people. That might not seem like a lot to you, but it's not as though I am some famous person who draws in thousands every time I speak. To teach this to hundreds of people means at most 50 at a time and often just one or two. You see, I am just a man, just a guy. At any rate, having taught this to people who are dating (it's been two years for me), those who are engaged

(I thought about it pretty seriously once), and those who are married (once thought I knew who I would marry; maybe I thought that way several times. That's immaturity for you), I have come to see many blessed. I have seen dating relationships end until God could be the focus. I have seen engagements honor God in purity. I have seen married couples rejuvenated and encouraged. I am now convinced though my initial motives in putting this on paper may have been a wife, it is now for you that I write these things down. I may or may not ever be married but that is not important. I have a responsibility, an obligation, to teach those things of God, those great truths. I am bound to share them with others and cry out like Paul did, "woe is me if I do not preach the gospel" **(1 Corinthians 9:16)**. I wish I could sit down with each of you face-to-face and share with you all God is putting on my heart these days. I am truly blessed. As you read these notes you can catch glimpses of me. Most of the stories mentioned, most of the feelings I describe, are mine. Each one entwined with a tender, and painful in some cases, memory. I have learned much and am blessed that I can share these things with you. Though you read these notes all as one work, they are in truth many small works put together over time. I have thought often of dating each different part to see the progression I have made over time; you will just have to take my word that progression has taken place in my life. Some of these things are new to me in the last few months; some are birthed through the culmination of hours of prayer and thoughtful meditation of scripture and God's design for our lives. Now I begin the undertaking of adding another fifteen pages or so to that which I had already; it is always an exciting prospect. I will spend hours on the computer working to adequately tell that which God has told me. I do pray these notes will bless you in your Godward pursuit. May you deeply desire God's love and may you be adept in making His love evident to others, be they a stranger, a friend, a family member, or your spouse. My love to God first, then to you.

Desiring God,
ryan

IF YOU HAVE NOT LOVE

Do you have love? I don't mean to ask if there is someone in your life that loves you and that you love in return. What I mean is, are you a person of love? Do you know what it means to love? I know, I know, we would like to think we all know what it means to love others. We think of our parents, our spouse, our kids, our best friends, or even our pets, and we think we really love them. What if I told you unless you had love in your life—pouring out from your heart and off your lips—you were nothing? Most of us wouldn't be concerned, would we? We would look briefly inward, decide we truly did know what it meant to love, pat ourselves on the back, and move on. Some of you would be offended a bit, thinking of those moments you weren't very loving, and you would object to my statement about being nothing in the absence of love. Let us look at a few verses.

"If I speak with the tongues of men and of angels, but do not have love, **I have become a noisy gong or a clanging cymbal**. And if I have the gift of prophecy, and know all mysteries and all knowledge; and if I have all faith, so as to remove mountains, but do not have love, **I am nothing**. And if I give all my possessions to feed the poor, and if I deliver my body to be burned, but do not have love, **it profits me nothing**." **1 Corinthians 13:1-3**

I wouldn't exactly say these verses are encouraging to us, but I would say they are a warning to the arrogant and puffed-up heart of men everywhere. Sure, we go through our lives convinced we know how to love, but you will notice in these verses it says without love, "I am a noisy gong or a clanging cymbal.... I am nothing.... It profits me nothing." These things being said, we should not look to our hearts to see if we truly know love, but we should look to the Bible. With the word of God as our standard, we can look into our hearts to see if we really love people.

From these verses we learn even if we are endowed with some of what Paul refers to as the greatest spiritual gifts but are absent from love, we amount to nothing. Nothing! Wow! That means if I am gifted with prophecy and can understand all mysteries and all knowledge and can by faith move a mountain out of my way, and even though people may think those things make me great, if love is missing, I am nothing. If I give all I have to the poor and if I submit my body to martyrdom but do so without love in my heart, it has profited me nothing. All our spiritual gifts are robbed of their power if not seasoned and permeated with love. All our self-denial, humility, and serving are worthless without love. If you are a doctor and by your knowledge and understanding you are able to help a person feel better, yet you did so without love, all your work amounts to nothing. This is not my opinion; it is God's. If you are a preacher and you preach the word of God every week and every week men come into a relationship with God, but you do this without love, you are nothing! I think for the most part all people want their lives to count for something—to be for something. We can be certain our lives will never amount to anything unless we first know what it is to love. If we are filled with love, all we do will matter and our lives will be much more than nothing; our lives will show the world the heart of God. For love comes from Him first, and when it is seen in us, we are in essence pointing people to the God who has taught us love.

So you think you know what love is? Ok. But be certain! Examine yourself and your view of love compared to the Bible's view of love. Look through these following pages to see what the Bible has to say about love and make sure you yourself are a lover of God and men.

I pray these notes would be an encouragement and a challenge to you and that they would help to improve your daily life. May God bless you deeply as you read and understand.

CHAPTER TWO

GOD LOVES ME, SO I LOVE HIM BACK

THE LOVE OF GOD FOR MAN
1 JOHN 4: 19

"We love because He first loved us." It is interesting, and we will cover this later, that so many people believe they are capable of love without God's intercession. This is a fallible idea, one that does not stand up to Scripture, the very word of God. If we are going to grasp love at its truth, as well as live and implement it in our lives, we must first understand that God Almighty loves us.

In the beginning God loved man. Ok, so the Bible does not say that when you open it up to the first page of Genesis. But keep looking. God created. And created. And created. God kept on creating until He was pleased with all He had made. If you look, you will find you are also one of the creations He is well pleased with. You and I have been made in

His image; look at what the Psalmist says in **Psalm 139:13-16.**

> For Thou didst form my inward parts; Thou didst weave me in my mother's womb. I will give thanks to Thee, for I am fearfully and wonderfully made; wonderful are Thy works, and my soul knows it very well. My frame was not hidden from Thee, when I was made in secret, and skillfully wrought in the depths of the earth. Thine eyes have seen my unformed substance; and in Thy book they were all written, the days that were ordained for me, when as yet there was not one of them.

I hope someone has shown you this passage already, perhaps dozens of times. Do you see what this text says? It tells of God creating your inmost parts. It talks of God knitting you together, making you wonderful! It goes on to say God knows all the days of your life and of mine. Now for those who have never before been exposed to the truth revealed in this Psalm, you may need to pause and enjoy the moment. Some of you read those previous lines without even batting your eye. Heck, you've heard it all before, and unless it is new and striking, you don't think it's something you should spend your time thinking about. Well, for people like you, and you know who you are, I have an ace up my sleeve. **Isaiah 40:12** says, "Who has measured the waters in the hollow of his hand, or with the breadth of his hand marked off the heavens?" It's a great verse, but you being ever the skeptic, ever in search of some great thing you've never heard before, ever believing that old truth cannot help the new you, for you I have a surprise. This verse talks about the size of God's hand. Look at the verse again. It says God's hand is so large all the waters fit in the hollow—or the cupped palm—of his hand. Even that description does not fully disclose the size of God's hand; it goes on to say the breadth of his hand, the part from thumb to pinkie, measures off the entire heavens. Well, according to science, the heavens are billions of light years across. Wow!! God's hand is huge! I have often said if God's hand is billions of light years across, just imagine how tall he is. Now with this fact in mind, I want you to take a moment to look at your fingerprints. Really study them. Look at the pattern. Keep in mind no one else in the entire world has fingerprints like yours. Sure, some of you just want to keep on reading, but you'll be doing yourself a real favor if you will stop to look for a few seconds. Here is the kicker: The God who is as big as ever, the very God Isaiah speaks of, is the very God who created you. Genesis tells us God formed you with His hands; the massive hand of God, who can hold the entire universe in His palm, is the very hand that fashioned you and took the time to carve into the tips of your fingers your own unique identity. So you see God does love you. I want for that to wow you the way it did me when I first understood it. But it doesn't end there.

Have you ever really looked at the last night of the life of Christ? Be careful not to just skim over this as you have so many times before. Really think on these things and experience in your heart the truth of the suffering Christ experienced for you. Several hundred people arrested Him in a garden. (**John 18:3**) All of His friends ran away. (**Mark 14:50**) Jesus went through several midnight trials; He was blindfolded as men stood around Him striking His face. "Tell us who is hitting you," they would cry out. (**Luke 22:63,64**) Beaten, He ended up in front of Pilate who wanted nothing to do with this Jesus of Nazareth. Almost in an effort to get the Jews to leave Jesus alone, Pilate had Him flogged. (**John 19:1**) Jesus Christ, God Almighty, was stripped naked and tied to a post, His back pulled tight. There Jesus was severely beaten by a whip with bits of rock and bronze and shards of pottery tied into the end. This beating bruised the body of Christ and ultimately ripped it to shreds. It is said often in this type of beating, the cheeks or ears will be ripped or torn. Soldiers put a purple robe on Jesus, a crown of thorns was pushed into His head, and a wooden staff was placed in His hand. The men gathered around mocking and spitting in His face; one took the staff and struck Jesus on the head. (**Matthew 27:27-31**) He was lead to Golgotha where they laid Him on a cross and drove nails deep in His hands and feet. When the nails were driven into a man's hands, it is said the arms would burn as if on fire and the fingers would curl in agony. It think it's interesting; the hand of God who holds the universe, the hand of God that formed you and me and gave us our fingerprints, this hand of God was crippled on the cross for you. For we know that everything that has ever been created was created by Jesus Himself. (**John 1:3,10; Colossians 1: 13-17**) So we see that He who created all things also laid down His life for us. When Jesus died He was laid in a tomb. (**John 19: 38-42**) But still, this is not the end. Three days later Jesus rose from the dead, that you and I might also not die but live with God forever. (**Matthew 28**) You see God does love you. He loved us while we were unlovable. He loved us while we were still sinners and separated from Him. It wasn't while we were doing "good" things that He died for us, rather "He demonstrates His love for us in that while we were yet sinners, Christ died for us." (**Romans 5:8**) We have to ask ourselves this question:

THE QUESTION:

Can we really love without first understanding that there is no love outside of God?

THE ANSWER REVISITED:

You see, "Every good and perfect gift comes down from the Father of heavenly lights who does not change like shifting shadows" (**James 1:17**). Jesus Himself told His disciples there was no one good except God (**Luke 18:19**). We are told love comes from God and, in fact, that God is love (**1 John 4:7, 16**).

If today you find yourself reading this and you are not a Christian—if you have not given your life over to God—then the Bible says you cannot know love (**1 John 4:7**). This is better understood when we look at Scripture and find we are, by our very nature, objects of wrath (**Ephesians 2:3**). Further, we are, apart from a relationship with Jesus, enemies of God (**Romans 5:10**). As enemies, we do not have love for God; rather, the Bible is clear that we hate Him. We tend to think that we carry within ourselves some innate goodness but that simply is not true. We find that the Bible teaches that no one is good or righteous or seeking God. (**Romans 3:10-12, Psalm 14:1-3, Psalm 53:1-3**) So we seem to be people who, if we have nothing good in us and if we cannot seek God, are destined for destruction.

But take heart, do not be discouraged, for while you may be an enemy of God and one that stirs up His wrath now, it will only take a moment to tell you of God's love for you, and soon you will know how to love, because you will know the Father of love! Remember that it was while you were in such a state as this that God sent Christ to die for you.

If today you know Jesus as your Lord, your Savior, stay with me, for this is the first step in becoming a first-rate lover.

"For God so loved the world that He gave His only son, that whoever believed on Him, would not die, but have eternal life" (**John 3:16**). "This is how God showed his love among us: He sent his one and only Son into the world that we might live through Him. This is love: not that we loved God, but that he loved us and sent his Son as an atoning sacrifice for our sins" (**1 John 4:9,10**). You see, God will not long endure sin in His presence without pouring out His wrath, and since we all have sinned (**Romans 3:23**), God could not patiently endure our sin forever. In fact, because of our sin the Bible says we deserve death. Nevertheless, God loved you and me so much, and so wanted to have His glory revealed in His creation, that He gave us a gift of eternal life (**Romans 6:23**).

This gift was Jesus Christ! Almost 2000 years ago, God sent His son Jesus to pay for our sins. Someone had to die for them because without the shedding of blood there can be no forgiveness, and that someone was Jesus. (**Hebrews 9:22**) He subjected himself to persecution, which included beatings, a flogging, and being hung to suffocate on a cross, held there by nine-inch nails in His wrists and His feet. There Jesus cried out, "It is finished!" And so it was. Jesus died, was laid in a tomb, and miraculously rose to life three days later. His death and resurrection was so that you might overcome death by the power of God. And all this because "God so loved the world." Some may tell you—you may believe it yourself—that there are those who do not know God as Lord and Savior, but still know love. My friends, if you do not know the very God from whom love comes, if you have not held the nail-scarred hand that love has eternally existed in, you cannot know love. There are many today that know the Origin of love, but do not understand it. Love is not a feeling, but an experience. When you stand next to a fire you feel its warmth; if you stand in the fire you experience it. There is such a striking contrast to warming your hands by the fire and to experiencing the burn, that you could hardly put it into words. It is time to move past head knowledge of the love of God, and really experience the fire of it. Decide today to experience

God's love for you. If you do that, you are at a place where you can love others rightly. How can you be a sufficient vessel of God's love for others if you yourself are not in the fire of it?

Today if you want God to be ruler over your life, "Confess with your mouth, 'Jesus is Lord,' and believe in your heart that God raised Him from the dead, and you will be saved" (**Romans 10:9**). "Confess" here means "to agree with." That is to say that we "agree with God that Jesus Christ is Lord." Of course, "Lord" would mean "master." You must agree with God that Jesus is Master of your life. Second, you must believe that God has raised Jesus from the dead; if Jesus was not raised from the dead, neither then will we be raised from the dead (**1 Corinthians 15:12-14**). "If anyone acknowledges that Jesus is the Son of God, God lives in him and he in God" (**1 John 4:15**). More simply (and the way I was taught as a child): just ask Jesus to come into your heart to live. Ask Jesus to be the Savior from death and the Boss of your life. Congratulations! That is the single most important decision you can ever make. If you have just done this for the first time please find a trustworthy pastor that you can share this with and from whom you can receive further counseling. Now, on to being the vessel of God!

THE LOVE OF MAN FOR GOD

We can hardly expect God to love us so greatly without requiring that we reciprocate on some level; yet I find very often we are guilty of just that. We tend to think since God has demonstrated His love to us while yet sinners, we are free from obligation; if God loved us as sinners such that He would have Christ die for us, we must be free from duty to love in return. This is near blasphemous! Rather, since God has loved us so completely, we make every provision to love Him with a deep love. I am far from an expert on what it means to love God with a deep love. Still, I know we are held to this. I know the Spirit within us, having come from God, desires nothing but to honor God. So in light of God's great love for us, let us consider what it means to love the Lord our God "with all your heart, all your soul, all your mind, and all your strength" (**Mark 12:30**). It would be easy for me to write four or five detailed sermons about all of these points, but I will try to refrain from that, lest I digress from the topic of these notes (this book?) and lose your interest. At best, I will offer a bit of detail, a bit of expansion, on each of these and will sum them up into one idea. I will be careful not to get carried away.

WITH ALL YOUR HEART:

"Watch over your heart with a   nce, for from it flows the springs of life."   **4:23** NAS

"Guard your heart above all els   e wellspring of life." **Proverbs 4:23** NIV

"As in water face reflects face, so the heart of man reflects man." **Proverbs 27:19** NAS

"Where your treasure is there your heart will be also." **Matthew 6:21** NIV

"Then the LORD saw that the wickedness of man was great on the earth, and that every intent of the thoughts of his heart was only evil continually." **Genesis 6:5** NAS

"For out of the heart comes evil thoughts, murders, adulteries, fornications, thefts, false witness, slanders." **Matthew 15:19** NAS

"The good man out of the good treasure of his heart brings forth what is good; and the evil man out of the evil treasure brings forth what is evil; for his mouth speaks from that which fills his heart." **Luke 6:45** NAS

No wonder we are told to guard our hearts above all else. Truly, our heart is the very wellspring of life yet its natural intents are towards wickedness all the time. (**Jeremiah 17:9**; **Genesis 6:5**) If we are going to love God with all of our heart, we must purge from it all that does not belong to God. One sure way to do so is to make God your greatest treasure. Whatever your treasure may be, that is what your heart is set on. (Note the verse listed above.) If your greatest value is money, fame, a job, romance, a car, or whatever, that is where your heart will be. Make sure you value God above all else. Don't just say you do, that part is easy. Really evaluate your life and discern if God is your treasure. Then vehemently guard your heart; do not let it get carried away by that lovely individual, or by prospects of a great future. Let your heart chase after God alone. Only then will you understand what it means to love God with all your heart. If your treasure is anything other than God, you are no different from the world, for truly the entire world seeks after things that are not eternal.

WITH ALL YOUR SOUL:

The soul. Somewhat mysterious isn't it? What exactly is it? What is its influence on us? I have a theory as to what the soul of man is. Everyone has a soul, but have you noticed it seems to be the only eternal part of a man? We know our bodies do not escape this earth, yet the soul goes on forever. We must look at that which all men have in common; the very thing all men have that is eternal in its nature. I contend that God alone is eternal in nature, and only things that come from God can find their way through eternity. If you look back on the creation account, you will see after God formed man, He breathed His breath in him. The breath of God, then, is in every man. The breath of God must be eternal, for it comes from Him. We know also that there is great importance in the breath of God, for "if He should determine to do so, if He should gather to Himself His spirit and His breath, all flesh would perish together and man would return to dust" (**Job 34:14-15** NAS). So then, the soul of man is that eternal part of him which will never fade away. Because it is so, we are told not to fear man who can harm the body, but rather to fear God who has the ability, after destroying the body, to destroy the soul in hell (**Matthew 10:28**). Further, we are asked to consider what it is worth to us if we gain everything in this age yet forfeit our soul, or what would we give in exchange for our soul (**Matthew 16:26**). If we are going to love God with our soul, we must examine that part of us which has always been eternal (again, I contend that it is perhaps the very breath of God), and put it to the service and glorification of our Father who is in heaven.

WITH ALL YOUR MIND:

What does it mean to love God with your whole mind? I think it's summed up for us quite well in scripture:

"If then you were raised with Christ, seek those things which are above, where Christ is, sitting at the right hand of God. *Set your mind on the things above not on the things of earth.*" (**Colossians 3:1-2** emphasis mine)

"Therefore *gird up the loins of your mind*, be sober... as obedient children, not conforming yourself to the former lusts... but be holy in all your conduct for it is written, 'Be holy as I am holy'." (**1 Peter 1:13-16** emphasis mine)

"*For those who live according to the flesh set their minds on the things of the flesh*, but those who live according to the Spirit, the things of the Spirit." (**Romans 8:5** emphasis mine)

So you see that our mind is supposed to be decidedly different from the mind of the world. I use "mind" in a singular sense simply because there is one mind of the world and one mind of the Spirit. The mind of the world is never set on the things of God, and the mind of the Spirit is never set on anything but God. Be certain we as believers are to have the mind of the Spirit. Further, we as believers already have the mind of Christ (**1 Corinthians 2:16**)! Since we know these things to be true, for us to love God with all our minds is to live according to the mind of the Spirit. Now there are all types of reasons we need to love God with our whole mind. I will list them for you and let you examine them on your own time.

1. To know God's will. (**Romans 12:2**)
2. Because a mind set on the world is enmity toward God. (**Philippians 3:17-19**)
3. To have and know peace. (**Romans 8:6, Isaiah 26:3**)

So we see that if we are loving God with our minds we will know His will for our lives, which is something most of us would love to know. Second, we find that if our mind is set on the things of the world then that is hatred toward God. Third, we are given supernatural peace when we set our minds on God's things. If you are still having a hard time learning what it means to love God with all of your mind then let me add one last thought. Think things that are true, honorable, right, pure, lovely, good, excellent, and praiseworthy. (**Philippians 4:8,9**) When you set your minds on such things as these you will be much closer to loving God with your mind.

WITH ALL YOUR STRENGTH:

I think while this could include or imply our emotional strength, or the fortitude with which we press on day by day, really it is an indication we are to love God with the strength of our body, that in the very actions of our body we are strong. Even in that,

I suppose, it does not mean the muscular capacity of a man or woman, but rather an indication of how one lives. Take, for example, this statement: "He shows great strength." This could indicate muscular strength or strength of presence. I believe "with all your strength" is an indication of the latter. I believe emotion and will are tied up in "with all your heart," and thoughts and perceptions are tied up in "with all your mind." Let us consider where our strength lies, and having shared some verses with you, I will need to give no further teaching on the matter.

"The weakness of God is stronger than man's strength." (**1 Corinthians 1:25** NIV)

Jesus has given us strength. (**1 Timothy 1:12**)

God is able to give us strength. (**2 Timothy 4:17**)

When we serve, we ought to do so in the strength that God has given. (**1 Peter 4:11**)

By faith our strength comes forth out of our weakness. (**Hebrews 11:34**)

Clearly these things aren't speaking of our muscle tone. Love Him with all that you have within you.

LOVE BY OBEDIENCE

Here is the sum of all things pertaining to our love for God: If we do not obey God, we do not love Him. Or rather, and probably more accurate, if we really love God we will be driven to obey Him by the love for Him that lives within us.

"If you love Me you will keep My command-ments." (**John 14:15** NAS)

"He who has My commandments and keeps them, it is he who loves Me..." (**John 14:21** NAS)

"Jesus answered and said to him, 'If anyone loves Me, he will keep My word; and My Father will love him, and We will come to him, and make Our abode with him. He who does not love Me does not keep My words; and the word which you hear is not Mine, but the Father's who sent Me.'" (**John 14:23-24** NAS)

Look how within ten verses, Christ mentions four times if we are to love Him, we must obey Him. How has God called us to obey Him? He has most certainly called us to love our neighbor as ourselves. Still, before I go there, let me wrap up this section on the love of man for God by sharing two last verses: "For *this is the love of God,* **that we keep His commandments**; and His commandments are not burdensome" (**1 John 5:3** NAS emphasis mine). "And this is love, that we walk according to His commandments. This is the commandment, just as you have heard from the beginning, that you should walk in it." (**2 John 6**)

WHO WAS MY NEIGHBOR AGAIN?

"'What commandment is the foremost of all?' Jesus answered, 'The foremost is, Hear, O Israel! The LORD our God is one LORD; and you shall love the LORD your God with all your heart, and with all your soul, and with all your mind, and with all your strength. The second is this, *You shall love your neighbor as yourself.* There is no other commandment greater than these'" (**Mark 12:28-31** NAS emphasis mine). We understand God loves us and we have looked at what it means to love God. Now the rest of the pages you have sitting before you will examine what it means to love others. Remember, Jesus implies all men are our neighbors in **Luke 10**. Further, I want you to think about what loving others means to us and the great commission found in **Matthew 28:19,20** "By this all men will know that you are My disciples, if you have love for one another" (**John 13:35** NAS). So there it is. Let us begin to dive into what it means to love others. We will start with misconceptions about love. Many of these I mention will speak to marriage, but a few can cross over to our daily lives.

CHAPTER THREE

MISCONCEPTIONS

ACME LOVE

There are, I think, a few misconceptions concerning love today. The reason that we so often have false views of love and fail to do it as it should be done is because more often than not we take our expectations of love back to what man calls love, rather than find our expectations for love grounded in the true and living God. As long as we try to love according to our standards we will fail. It is only when I come to learn what love means through the eyes of God that I have a hope of loving others well. I called this section "acme love" because of the coyote and roadrunner cartoons. Coyote was always trying to catch and eat the roadrunner. Coyote would always get products from acme designed to serve a purpose, but every time, we as the viewer could be certain the product would backfire or fail to work in the way the coyote expected. The catapult intended to fling him onto the roadrunner would instead flip over smashing the poor coyote into the ground. The rocket shoes would go out of control and fly him off a cliff. Certainly the coyote should have quit using such flawed products for they never accomplished what they were intended to accomplish. In a similar fashion, you and I have been taught things about love that simply are not correct. We keep buying into false ideas and principles about love believing that they will help us reach our goal, and we find ourselves time and time again entrenched in failure. We have accepted these things as truth and are doomed to the same disastrous results the generations before us have experienced if we do not learn to distinguish between misconceptions and truth. There are even men in our pulpits today who are guilty of counseling culturally rather than biblically when it comes to love.

1. Love is **NOT** a roller coaster ride! In fact, no area of life is to be depicted by a roller coaster swinging up and down, and throwing you side to side. Oh sure, you may feel that way every so often. Circumstances are hard sometimes. But God is not thrown off by anything happening in our lives, and after all, this life is not about us anymore, but about God. Furthermore, love IS NOT a plateau that levels out at some point. With the kind of strength and stability that comes from a Sovereign God, no part of our life should seem like a roller coaster. Rather, our life should be like that described in **Psalm 84:7** and several other places in the Bible. **Psalm 84: 7** — "They go from strength to strength, until each appears before God

in Zion." The "they" mentioned in this verse is the pilgrim from verse five that finds his strength in God. We are to go from strength to strength, from better to better, with God. **2 Corinthians 3: 18** —"But we all, with unveiled face, beholding as in a mirror the glory of the Lord, are being transformed into the same image from glory to glory…" (NKJ). Or consider **Romans 1: 17**—"For in it the righteousness of God is revealed from faith to faith…" (NKJ). Where in that formula is there room for a roller coaster or desert plateau? God is about our growth and transformation into the likeness of His son Jesus. God is conforming us to the image of Jesus. Since God is love, that is to say that there is no love that exists outside of God, we cannot rightfully say that love is a roller coaster ride. We cannot approach love so callously as to say "I just don't love them like I used to," or "they don't deserve my love today," or even "I just don't feel the same love for them." Love is of God and as such it is strong and steady. Such shortcomings on our part are just that, shortcomings! Press on to let your love grow day by day.

2. Love is **NOT** a feeling. I have already expressed in the introduction that love is an experience. Sometimes I feel like ice cream; sometimes I feel sad. Sometimes I feel like doing something with you; often I feel like going fishing. A feeling is typically based on circumstance or condition. It is like an IF-THEN statement in computer programming. Most often we say "IF you will do this or

that THEN I will love you more or better." Love is not that way. Love is. That's all. Love comes from God and God called himself I AM, so love IS. It exists because God exists. Love is not something that can occur in my heart without God's help. Whether you choose to obey God by loving others is up to you. But it is not your choice to love. God wrote that into the program. Maybe it looks something like this:

SINCE: God THEN: Love — — — — —-

God will always BE. He does not change! His love for me will not change based on my performance today. His love for me will not wax and wane based on how nice I am today. How exciting it is that love will always be; that it is not based on condition or circumstance! So we ought not base our love for others on how we feel about them today. Rather we ought to love in the same manner as God loves us. How terrible, how wretched, and sad it is when people cannot look at my life and see the eternal nature of God's love and how it's not based on feeling. Love is **NOT** a feeling.

3. Love can**NOT** fail. I'm going to tell you something different than anything you have ever heard before. Many people will tell you marriage is so hard; you are going to fight and bicker and be upset with each other. You have been told heated words will be exchanged and doors will be slammed. What is so sad is you have come to expect it. I do not think anyone gets married and expects

anything different than this. But love CANNOT fail. Remember God has the patent on love, not you. Sure, if you owned love, if you had invented it, there would be glitches and problems. You would have to offer some kind of money-back guarantee, or a two for one special on faulty love. But guess what, God is love, it is His design and it cannot fail. You do not have to settle for difficulty in love or bitter arguments. You do not have to settle for slamming doors; God has worked out all the bugs of love. It is in perfect working order, and you got it free of charge in the "Jesus Christ is my Savior" package. God is unfailing; so is His love. Love is infinitely deep and wide. There is no room for error. I once taught the pages you are now reading over the course of a weekend. After I was done with the seminar the preacher who had invited me said "you did a good job, but I just feel that you are a bit idealistic in how love works. It is really hard." He then proceeded to tell me how just the other day when he was driving down the road with his wife and baby and the baby was crying and his wife was talking about something, and how he just stopped and yelled "SHUTUP! JUST SHUTUP!" He smiled as he said "it's just not always like you preach it." I wanted to stop him and tell him how what he had done was an outburst of anger and how it was not loving. It wasn't that God's love had failed. It wasn't that love somehow didn't rise to the occasion. It was that this man had failed to show forth God's enduring love. That is the real issue. Love never fails. You can be confident that all failure rests squarely on the human heart and not on the love that has its start in our eternal God. Now we just need to learn what His love looks like. Hang on, we're almost there.

4. Love canNOT change overnight. There will not be more love tomorrow than there is today. Love is not going to change shape, or blow up, or melt away. Have you ever heard someone say, "I fell in (or out of) love with him or her overnight"? It doesn't happen that way (most likely the one who says something like this has never really grasped love). No! Love does not change, but our understanding of it does. Let me give you what, I hope, will be a helpful illustration. Chess is a game I enjoy, although I am not very good at it. It has been around for a long time, about 1400 years. The rules are set and it is only chess when you follow the rules. Now, suppose I see a chessboard for my first time, but all I know is the knight moves in an L shape; I am not going to be able to sit down and play chess. But say tonight I study all the rules, and tomorrow I sit down at a chessboard and know how all the pieces move and even some of the special moves like en passant and castling. The game of chess never changed; it did not grow. What changed was my understanding of the game, and with an understanding of the board and the pieces, I am able to practice what has already been. In **1 John**, we are told that not only is love from God, but in fact, God is love.

It therefore stands to reason if God is love and love is from Him, the ability to love hinges on the understanding of that. We must realize that God, as love, has made Himself available to us. The more we understand of God, the more we understand of love. The more we understand of love, the better we can put into practice what has always been.

5. You can**NOT** fall in love. Now, I am sure on this point many will argue with me. But, as we've just said, love is an understanding of who God is. That type of understanding is not something you realize as you look across the crowded room and lock eyes with the most beautiful creature in the entire world. That type of understanding does not come when he brings flowers, or when she gives you that smile, or because the world melts with your first—or thirtieth—kiss. Falling in love is a phrase giving the idea that you tripped on a crack in the sidewalk and fell face first into something you were surprised to find. This is not love. Feeling, perhaps; infatuation, almost definitely. But it is not love. In order to love, we must understand the love of God and that comes from knowing God. It is not tripping or stumbling into love, but a growing understanding of the nature of God. As you grow to know God more, you will love better. But it will not be something you fall into. It will be something you study and practice and discipline yourself to live out. We don't fall in love by accident. We learn more about how God

loves and we purposefully put that in the practical day to day living out of our lives. Let me add a text that I hope will help illustrate this point. "For this reason, I bow my knees before the Father that He would grant you to be strengthened with power through His Spirit in the inner man; so that Christ may dwell in your hearts through faith; and that you, being rooted and grounded in love, may be able to comprehend with all the saints what is the height and depth, and to know the love of Christ which surpasses knowledge, that you may be filled up with the fullness of God." (**Ephesians 3:14-19**) So we see then that it is not by accident that we come to know God's love for us. Rather, through much prayer, by the power of the Spirit of God, having already been grounded in the love of God, we are finally able to understand the greatness of God's love. Only through that process will we ever be able to love others rightly. It takes us being "filled up with the fullness of God" to love others and that is never something we casually fall in to.

6. You can**NOT** "make" love. In television and on the movie screen today, you see many people entangled in a naked sweaty pile and they call it "making love". Most often this couple, having united their bodies in a way God only intended for a man and wife, were on their first date, didn't know each other's names, or were just caught up in passionate lust. We tend to glorify this kind of behavior and yet clearly it is an abomination to

God. How do we glorify it, you ask? Well, if I might be so bold, I would answer that by viewing it so lightly and thinking so little about it we glorify that which God calls wickedness. Sexual intercourse outside of the marriage bed can never be deemed as "making love," since love is of and from God. And God takes no delight in sexual behavior other than that which is shared between a man and his wife. Further, even in the holy, God-ordained confines of marriage, sex is not "making love." God has given a man and wife not only the opportunity, but the honor, of delighting in each other's bodies. But no act of sexual relation can "make" that which only comes from God and has existed from all eternity. You may argue my point is moot or simply semantics, but I believe we take too lightly the things of God. We can indeed demonstrate the things of God in our lives, including love. We can indeed, in the context of marriage, see a man and woman physically coupled together in an effort to not only fulfill marital obligation, but more importantly to delight in and demonstrate love to one another. Any other sexual relation that exceeds the bounds of marriage is tawdry and filthy in the sight of God, and is absent of even a hint of the love that would come from Him. Still my emphasis in these pages is to compel you to think of love as that which comes from God alone and has always been a part of His character. That being true we cannot "make" love for love is of God, yet we can show forth His great love to others.

WHAT GOOD IS A CLAY JAR?

You may not know this, but you are a vessel. If Jesus is your savior, then you have everything you need to live life and be godly for you are a coheir with Jesus. (**2 Peter 1:3,4; Romans 8:16,17**) You have the surpassing treasure of Christ inside of you! (**2 Corinthians 4:7**) Look, it is right there in all its beauty; right there inside you! You are the clay jar, the vessel. And just what does that mean? Just what are you good for? You were made specifically to pour out the things of God into our world. Now, in this book I have only endeavored to write about love and since God has poured out His unfailing love into your life and since you live in this world, then pour, baby, pour. It's what you're good for!

CHAPTER FOUR

FOUNDATIONS AND CORNERSTONES:

I hope you're comfortable, because now we begin with what love is. What we will be covering in this section is actually (in my opinion) the foundation of everything else we will cover. My hope is that after you finish going through the Foundations and Cornerstones of love, you will see people, and the way you treat them, a little differently. I hope to lay out in a practical way a definition of love, which you will find easy to understand. I will tell you now that when I began this study on love, I thought I already had a pretty good grip on it. I was SO WRONG! When God began to define what love was, my spirit was broken and I despised the way I treated others. For the first time, I realized I did not love people like I should, like we all should. When God shows us truth and we see the lies in our lives that we have accepted as truth, we are disgusted. I was pretty gross. But now that you're all excited, pumped up, and ready to see if a monster is in you where love should be, let's go to **1 Corinthians 13:4-8**.

Love is patient, love is kind. It does not envy, it does not boast, it is not proud. It is not rude, it is not self-seeking, it is not easily angered, it keeps no record of wrongs. Love does not delight in evil but rejoices with the truth. It always protects, always trusts, always hopes, always perseveres. Love never fails.

There is one thing I should probably mention before we delve into these characteristics of love. We are to demonstrate Godliness in our lives. Since God is love, we are also to demonstrate characteristics of loveliness in our lives—in fact, we should demonstrate more than **characteristics** of loveliness, we should demonstrate **loveliness**, not in pieces, but in its fullness. After all, could we not also read the above passage as, "God is patient, God is kind, God does not envy..." and so on? I tell you this because it is not just a nice idea to follow the guidelines of love written out for us in Corinthians, but rather, it is expected of us. By demonstrating loveliness, we are demonstrating Godliness. Remember that we have already covered the fact that if we are not doing things out of love then we are nothing.

3-20-03

Hello, my beautiful wife. I want you to know as I look over these notes, I know I will have already failed you numerous times by the time you read this. I pray even now that God will teach me to be patient with you in all things. I endeavor through the strength of my Mighty God to show you all kindness. May I never extend to you any discourtesy. May my words always be used to strengthen you and to bless you. I seek to never envy those things God blesses you with, but to always call them the blessings of our God and rejoice with you in them. I will strive to never boast above you or to magnify myself to your hurt. I will seek to be humble with you in all things and to be your servant at all times, humbling myself at your feet and receiving your praise with the understanding that I have only done my duty as a husband. My Love, may you always be able to speak in truth of me that I have never been rude to you or made light of your role in my life. I will do my best—rather, I will seek to have God work in me His best—to never seek my own, but to always seek how I might bless you. I will not be easily angered and will never hold a grudge against you or bring up those things from our past. I will rejoice in truth only and will trust you explicitly. As a husband, I will do all I can to protect you in every way. Together, we will hope in eternity and my love for you will always persevere. I love you so much.

ryan

PATIENCE

Stop and reflect for just a moment on the patience of God. WOW!! He doesn't have to let me keep living. He didn't even have to save me out of my sin. I was His enemy. I was an object of wrath. Even in all that He demonstrated patience for me and saved me.

Stop and reflect for just a moment on the patience of Jesus. WOW!! Persecuted! Beaten! Forsaken! Crucified! And still full of patience!

Stop and reflect for just a moment on your patience. EEEWW!! If it's as bad as mine then you should really be bothered. I've been praying through this for years and I still am so impatient.

Did you know if you are impatient with someone in your words, you are not loving them? Did you know if you are impatient in your actions, you are not demonstrating love? Did you know if you are impatient in your thoughts, you are not living in God's unfailing love? The first part of **1 Corinthians 13** says that "love is patient." Do you see any room in that statement for any amount of impatience? Does it say "love is patient unless"? Anything less than patience in words, actions, or thoughts is simply not right! When I realized this, I felt sick to my stomach. Day in and day out, God showed me where I lacked in patience, where I lived outside of love. Patience is letting the lady with two kids cut in front of you at the super-market because she is busier than you are. Patience is letting one more car in front of you before you move on. Patience is when a friend shows up an hour late and you do not let it get under your skin. Patience is talking for an hour to the cell phone people for charging you for the internet service you never added to your plan, and all the while being gracious. We live in such a fast-paced society where there seems to be no room for patience. But impatience is sin, plain and simple, because it is less than the perfect love God has for people. Even now, I am praying for God to give me victory over impatience.

KINDNESS

"Love is kind." Just like patience, there is no room in that statement for anything less than kindness to be demonstrative of love. You may want to argue that it is not possible for you to be kind, or patient, or any of those other things all the time. I would say you're right. But it is possible for God to be kind and patient all the time, and, after all, you are no longer yours. (**1 Corinthians 6; 19, 20**) You belong to God and He is strong enough. Who is in control of your life right now? Who's supposed to be? Since we know, through Christ, the strength to be kind is available, how do we show kindness? When was the last time you invited someone you did not know to sit with you because they were sitting alone? When was the last time someone told you they were having a bad time and you called them later to see how they were doing? When was the last time someone asked you to pray for them and you forgot? We should draw those near who seem to have no one. If we are truly kind, we will want to check on someone who is hurting. If someone asks us to pray for them, we should do it immediately that they might be encouraged, then go home and remember to do it again. When we are kind, we will pay attention to others. When we are kind, we will bear up under the story that someone has told you "a thousand times."

I will give you a couple of examples from my own life I am not proud I have. I have three sisters, two of whom are considerably younger than I am. One is 12 years younger, one 15 years. Once when I was home for a college break, Jessie, the one 12 years my junior, woke me at about 7:00 in the morning to ask if she could crawl into bed with me. I was upset at having been woken and told her no. I told her to leave me alone and to bother someone else. How I wish now I had not done that; I love my sister, and am grateful for her and the way she shows me love. I was unkind to my sister. She was so sweet that once when she was at children's camp she bought me a wooden keychain with a name carved into it because she just loved me and wanted to give me a gift. Now my name is Ryan and the keychain was "Rosemarie" but it really was the thought that counted. She was just so kind and so often I was not. I cannot tell you how many times Lisa, the youngest, excitedly sat me down to tell a joke she had just learned. I would ruin the punch line because I had heard it before, and the joke lost its joy. I should have listened attentively and laughed like I had never before heard anything so funny; instead, I was unkind. Yet once when I was about 18 and Lisa was almost three, I was crying and she came and sat in my lap and asked me what was wrong and she hugged me. How kind she was. My third sister, Haley, is almost three years younger than me. I still have a valentine card that she sent me 12 years ago. The card just tells me how much she loves me. How kind she has been to me over the years and how unkind I've been to her.

One of the greatest ways I think we are unwittingly, and often deliberately, unkind is in the things we say. If I call one of my friends a "nerd" in jest, I have in my mind a picture of someone I would consider fills the qualities of a nerd. Whether I think about it or not, I classify someone as being less valuable or less accepted or less important than another. We do this all the time by using names such as dork, punk, nerd, slut, and many more. When we say it to someone's face we are unkind; when we say it behind someone's back we are unkind. Keep in mind that just because someone doesn't know you have been unkind doesn't mean you are free and clear. The Bible says "you shall not curse a deaf man, nor place a stumbling block before the blind." (**Leviticus 19:14**) The point being that even those things we do apart from someone's knowledge can still be sin. God does not view one person as less valuable than another. So often in our name-calling we tag someone as invaluable. This also is unkind. Do you regret being unkind, or is it that you know you are supposed to be kind that you regret?

ENVY

Envy, a green-eyed monster? Well, truth be told, I have blue eyes, and a monster... (Pause, Reflect)... no, I don't think so. I look normal enough, but have I ever envied? YOU BET! Envy is wanting something someone else has, and wishing they didn't have it. The Bible tells us love does not envy, therefore we are left no room to. In fact, we are told "envy rots the bones" (**Proverbs 14:30**). I'm not going to spend much time here, but that does not mean this is an area you can overlook. When was the last time you thought twice about something someone else had? For example: at work one day the person who does the same thing you do gets recognized for the same sort of thing you did a month ago. You think to yourself "man, he/she should not have gotten that; it's really not a big deal. Heck, I did the same thing a month ago. I should be the one recognized." (Total tangent: it's funny, but I cannot write about envy and give examples of it without twisting my face into a sour expression. Even the words in my head as I prepare to type them seem to come out onto the screen of this computer with bitterness and hate. No wonder "envy rots the bones.") Or what if you wake up one morning and head to the kitchen to find your roommate chomping down on the last bagel (or perhaps your corn pops). "Oh NO!" the voice in your head screams out. "I wanted that bagel." Later that day you scrounge through the fridge and find your-self thinking back to "the bagel that you should be eating," and you find yourself not loving. Whether you're envious at work—or simply have bagel envy—if you want something someone else has, such that it robs them of having it, you do not love. Instead, rejoice in their benefit and joy, after all your "reward is with God" (**Isaiah 49:4**). As a side note, if you still don't think envy is a big deal, you may be interested in knowing the reason that wicked men sought to put Jesus to death was because of envy. "... Because of envy they delivered Him up" (**Matthew**

27:18). "...The chief priests had delivered Him up because of envy" (**Mark 15:10**).

BOASTING

"Love does not boast." Boasting is saying something that will benefit you but not the person you are speaking to. "Let no unwholesome talk come out of your mouth but only what is helpful for the building up of others according to their needs that it may benefit all who listen" (**Ephesians 4:29**). It is important you not speak to build yourself up. We must question ourselves every time we want to tell a story. Are we looking for compliments? I have a preacher friend that once told me he would never ask someone if they enjoyed his message. He would not do this because in his spirit he found himself wanting them to say what a great job he had done. It was only after he quit asking for compliments and affirmations that he got them and was satisfied. When he would practically beg for a compliment and get one, he found it somewhat empty. What if they had only affirmed him because he had given them no choice? It is not "honorable to seek one's own honor" (**Proverbs 25:27**). "Humble yourselves before the Lord, and He will lift you up" (**James 4:10**). "Humble yourselves, therefore, under God's mighty hand, that *He* may lift you up in due time" (**1 Peter 5:6**). It is for God to lift up! Love does not boast. Actually, though, there is a time you can boast and be justified in doing so. The prophet Jeremiah tells us that he who boasts should boast about this: "that he understands and knows God," and that God is the "Lord, who exercises kindness, justice, and righteousness on earth" (**Jeremiah 9:23-24**). So, can you boast that you know God intimately, that you understand him? If not, it is imperative you watch what you say. We must realize that even our boasting in knowing God is not a boasting of my knowledge but rather a boasting as to the type of God that He is. If you look at Jeremiah 9 you will notice that the emphasis is on God and not on us. Let me end with one last verse. "But he who boasts, let him boast in the LORD. For not he who commends himself is approved, but whom the Lord commends." (**2 Corinthians 10:17,18**)

PRIDE

You know what I think? Pride very often precedes boasting. Remember the time you stopped to help someone who had run out of gas? You took them to the gas station and gave them a buck or two to put gas into their car. As soon as you dropped them off, you were busting at the buttons. Well, later that same day you see your friend and you cannot wait to tell them what you have done (you almost have to boast). You tell as many people as you can you were late because you stopped to help out a person in need. I'll let you know what I think. God did not care for the way the Babylonians lived, but when it came time for the people of Judah to be punished, God used the Babylonians to do it. In fact, the Bible tells us God called them His servants. God did not care for the lives the Pharisees lived, but he used them to bring about the crucifixion of Christ that we may have life. The Babylonians were idol worshippers and the Pharisees were religious hypocrites; both were quite proud of the things they had done, but they were used for His purpose. My point is this: the next time you get so big on yourself, stop to think. Perhaps God just used you to give one of His faithful and humble servants the hand He promised them. Next time you have an opportunity to be used by God, thank Him for giving you an opportunity to serve. I am almost certain it will keep you humble. Consider these verses.

"Everyone who is proud in heart is an abomination to the LORD; assuredly, he will not be unpunished." (**Proverbs 16:5**)

"God is opposed to the proud but gives grace to the humble." (**1 Peter 5:5, James 4:6**)

RUDENESS

"Love is not rude." It grieves me to point out that if we fully understood that love is not rude, we would be embarrassed and shamed by the way we treat others. But, I will not apologize for having to point it out. When God truly helped me to understand this, I was distressed at how rude I was in my actions, my words, and my thoughts to people. Who is it that we feel we can be rude to? After all, most of the people we are rude to we may never see again. Who is it that deserves our arrogance, our superiority, and our biting tongues? The grocer who over-charged us? The barber that cut your hair a little less than perfect? The person that drives too slowly on the highway, or the one who cuts you off in town? Your spouse must deserve it when you have already had a bad day. What about those phone surveys that call in the middle of dinner, or all of those long distance carriers that want your business? I praise God that I am writing this now. Earlier today I received an electric bill and was charged for two months of service. The previous balance was said to have been past due. Now, what is really interesting about this is that I have only lived in this apartment for one month. I think my natural tendency would be to be rude when I call to straighten this out tomorrow, but now I am very conveniently reminded to love. Truth be told, no one deserves our attitude. As to the grocer, have you ever added numbers wrong? The barber; have you ever had less than perfect hands? The slow person on the interstate; have you ever been trying to look at a map and figure out if you missed your exit? The one who cuts you off in town; what if they just got word their mother, husband, or child is in the hospital? And you think you have the right to be rude? Think of the example of compassion given us in Christ. How many times was He bothered at suppertime? How many times did He try to get away by Himself, only to be followed by scores of people? How many times was His forward step slowed to a crawl as people pushed their way to see Him, to hear Him, or to touch Him? How many times did He scowl and say, "I cannot feed these five thousand, I have not yet eaten." Or, "get away from me; this is my time and when I want you guys to follow me, I'll tell you. Quit asking for things. Quit touching me. I can't touch you, you disgust me; you may be contagious." He never did. No more than this, do we have reason to be rude.

SELF-SEEKING

"Love is not self-seeking." This is when you do something to receive something. It never ceases to amaze me how selfish we are. We always want to be first; we want to be first in line, we want the new album first, we want the new car, new shirt, new job, and we want them first. Or we want the last compliment by a peer, after-all, the last one will be remembered most. We want the last recognition at the banquet. We want to present our case last so we will be heard better. We want to pick the movie we want to see, eat at the restaurant we like. Sit where we want to sit and do what we want to do whenever we are pleased to do it. Boasting goes well with this one; it's like fishing for a compliment. Nevertheless, it goes beyond just boasting, but we will cover this more in a little while. Granted, most of us have learned conditional love so we tend to "do" in order to "get". Just remember Christ came for others, not for Himself. I think you will find that if you can live for the benefit and better-ment of others, it will be impossible to be rude, impa-tient, or unkind. "Do nothing out of selfish ambition or vain conceit, but in humility *consider others better than yourselves.* Each of you should look not only to your own interest, but also to the interest of others" (**Philippians 2:3-4** emphasis mine).

ANGER

If I had to pair the fact that "love is not easily angered" with one of the other characteristics we have already discussed, I would have to say it goes well with patience. What kind of things have you seen someone get angry over in the blink of an eye? Being easily angered is going from a perfectly good mood to hot rage in mere seconds. It took God hundreds of years to become so angry at the Israelites that He sent them into captivity in Assyria and Babylon; I have witnessed people throwing fits because of a look they were given. It's ridiculous. If you are one who gets easily angered, you are going to have a hard time letting others know of God's unfailing love. If you want to know when it is OK to get angry, I'll tell you: Christ was arrested late at night, given a midnight trial, blindfolded and hit in the face, struck on the head with a stick, had a thorny crown pushed onto his brow, flogged, and spit upon. He was hung on a cross and held by nails in His hands and feet; as He suffocated, he prayed, "Father, forgive them." Apparently, we need to go just past that point to be justified in our anger. Instead of anger, try praying for that person. Perhaps they have never seen the love of God. OK, so you're saying it was unfair for me to put the example of Christ before you. Let's try another. Stephen—you'll find his story in Acts 7—after brilliantly defending the gospel of Christ, was led outside amid shouting men and was stoned to death. Even as the stones were bruising and beating his body, he cried out, "Father, do not hold this sin against them." So you tell me, when is our anger justified? Perhaps it is only when people are disregarding God completely. Think about Jesus driving out of the temple all the moneychangers and merchants. When was the last time you were angry because someone spoke God's name in vain? For such things you are justified, but when spoken against you, there is no justification for anger. Perhaps we should be angry at the sin in our lives that keeps us from loving like we are supposed to. Here are some more verses for you to consider:

"He who is slow to anger has great understanding, but he who is quick-tempered exalts folly." **Proverbs 14:29**

"He who is slow to anger is better than the mighty, and he who rules his spirit, than he who captures a city." **Proverbs 16:32**

"…wise men turn away from anger." **Proverbs 29:8**

"Let everyone be quick to listen, slow to speak and slow to anger; for the anger of man does not achieve the righteousness of God." **James 1:19,20**

"…be angry and do not sin" **Ephesians 4:26**

RECORD OF WRONG

How good is your memory? What amazes me is that God, because of Christ, has forgiven and pardoned me. I once read that only God can both forgive and pardon. If you were sent to court and were pardoned for a crime, you were not found guilty so you don't need forgiveness. But if in the trial you are found guilty, you can be forgiven, but not pardoned from the consequences of your crime. God, however, has forgiven and pardoned us. Our records are clean and clear. Did you know God has provided pardon and forgiveness for everyone through Christ? That includes the person whose record of wrongs you have filled out in detail. If God holds no record on you, how can you on someone else? Why do you still hold fast to the wound that someone gave you twenty years ago or even yesterday? I am certain that it cannot be helpful to your life. It must stir up bitterness in you. Furthermore, it is not like the love of God that has seen our sins and our wrongs cast into the depth of the sea and removed from us as far as the east is from the west. (**Micah 7:18-20, Psalm 103:12**)

EVIL

"Love does not delight in evil." Do you find great satisfaction in things that are not of God? "Test everything. Hold on to the good. Avoid every kind of evil" (**1 Thessalonians 5:21-22**). I'll tell you this even though I know you've heard it before. Try to picture Jesus in an actual body right next to you. Then ask yourself, "Would He be here? Would He be doing this? Would He find this funny? Would He contribute to this conversation?" I tell you what, I have evil tendencies. I did not know they were evil until God began to teach me about renewing my mind. "Do not conform any longer to the pattern of this world, but be transformed by the renewing of your mind. Then you will be able to test and approve what God's will is— His good, pleasing and perfect will" (**Romans 12:2**). I do not think God Almighty would laugh at some of the "clean" jokes we tell. What about all the things we take time to look at, whether watching them or reading them? How many times have you sat looking at a movie screen, a TV screen, a magazine, or a book, and kept glancing over your shoulder to make sure no one else was in the room? How many times have you turned down your music when someone like your parent, your pastor, your youth minister, or a respected friend came into the room because the lyrics were vulgar? How many jokes have you told or stories have you shared that you first got up to close the door because you didn't want someone else to hear? If you've done these things, I would say you are finding pleasure in evil. It should be put away from you if you desire to live and love as God does. Love does not find joy in the things of this world; not even a little bit. Love holds on to the good. God wants you to be innocent of what is evil, but more than that if you really love Him you are supposed to hate what is evil. (**Romans 16:19, Psalm97:10**)

TRUTH

"Love rejoices in the truth." I think several things about this. One, love rejoices in God. Did Christ not say, "I am the way, the TRUTH, and the life" (**John 14:6**)? If Christ is THE TRUTH then when God's love is manifested in me I should be fully delighting in Christ Jesus my Savior. Second, I think that love rejoices in truth by not giving itself over to lying. When you love someone, you will not protect yourself with lies. Sometimes it is more than just not lying. Sometimes rejoicing in truth simply means to be honest. I have found I am being untruthful when I keep things to myself that would benefit or compliment others. For example, there was this girl I was once very attracted to. I did not know if this was someone God wanted me to date or not, but it was someone I spoke to from time to time. As my attraction toward this woman grew and as I continued to talk to her, I felt as though I was hiding things from her by not letting her know my feelings. It was important to me that whatever kind of relationship we built, it would be built on honesty. So, one day I gave her a call and told her. That girl and I never did date, but we are still excellent friends and we talk and encourage each other often. Truthfulness will draw others near to you. Finally, I think love rejoices over someone else being truthful with you. This is probably the hardest one. Sometimes my best friends will come to me and point out an area in my life that needs work. Unfortunately, my first reaction is to get defensive. Later, however, I rejoice that they came to me; I am trying to get to a place where my first reaction is to rejoice. I will open myself up a little more: there was a time I wanted to ask out this other girl. I called her up and was honest with her, and she was honest with me when she said she was not and had not been interested in me. But you know what? God had already begun to teach me to rejoice in truth, and so I did. That particular girl is one of my dearest and best friends and I talk to her every week. (In my final edit and years after the previous sentence was originally written I have to admit I don't even know who this person is anymore. Whoever it was we haven't talked in years. But we'll leave it in for the sake of illustration.) Now, on a level deeper than that of hearts set on romance, there will be times when we need to be rebuked or corrected and if we really love as we ought to, and if we really rejoice in truth, then I consider even that rebuke to be kindness. "Let the righteous [person] smite me in kindness and reprove me; it is like oil upon my head; do not let my head refuse it." **Psalm 141:5.** We also know that if someone is really our friend, then even the wounds they cause can be trusted. (**Proverbs 27:6**) Let us learn to rejoice in the truth that is God, and in being truthful, and in having others be truthful with us. There is love in it.

PROTECTION

What is there to say? It is important to protect others when we can. One way we can do this is to not tear others down. It is of vital importance that you do not criticize or make fun of strangers, acquaintances, friends, and especially your spouse. I have heard people say, and perhaps am guilty of it myself, "Let me tell you this story about so and so; they said it was OK." Have you ever asked someone's permission to share a humiliating or embarrassing story with someone else? I think this is something we all struggle with. People are telling funny stories and you have one, only it's about someone else, so you throw it in the conversation. You have failed to protect that person. I have seen pastors tell anecdotes in a sermon having to do with their wives. After the story, they are quick to say their "lovely wife" knew they were going to share the story because he had asked her permission earlier. I contend that we can better love and protect others by not only not asking permission, but by not even desiring to share a story that could hurt someone's feelings or cause them to be made uneasy. We do not protect when we contribute to their hurt. We can also put a stop to someone tearing down someone else. When was the last time you jokingly told whomever it was that cooked dinner, "what is this stuff, road kill?" Of course everyone at the table laughs, including the cook, but what is beyond the smile? Are you guilty of telling someone who may be very proud of their haircut, it looks like they got butchered? Be careful, little tongue, what you say. I think protection comes across in our attitudes, and I know it is born at the heart of us. I think it keeps your kids from seeing things they do not need to. (Parents, if you are not actively taking a part in your child's life and discerning the types of things they are doing and the kinds of friends they are associating with, then I put it to you that you are not loving your child well for you are not protecting them.) I think you are protecting someone when the group suggests a movie with an "R" rating and you pick one that is "PG." You protect someone when you are seeking the very best for him or her. Our tendency is to think of jumping literally in front of the bullet. But more often than not, it is the figurative bullet that others need protection from. Maybe your friend was going to make a decision that would be harmful to their walk with Christ, and you pointed it out to them. It is important to remember that "love always protects."

TRUST

I want you to know when the Bible tells us that "love always trusts," it is important to keep in mind we are not supposed to be stupid. God has given us each a measure of common sense. I will always warn people away from stopping to help a stranded car if they are alone. I do not mean for you to throw open the door to your house at 3:00 a.m. to the man who has said he badly needs help. Please be wise, but remember that love always trusts. Now, while I think that there are some practical ways by which we can put this to practice in our life, I really think that all of our trust should finally and ultimately rest in God. Do you trust God? Do you believe that He is who He says He is? "Put your trust in the light while you have it, so that you may become sons of light." **John 12:36.** We know that it is those of us who trust God that have our faith credited to us as righteousness. (**Romans 4:5**) Remember, love always trusts, and most often that is going to mean "in God".

HOPE

I once heard a pastor say that wishing was wanting something to happen. But when you hoped for something, you waited expectantly, knowing all the while it was on its way. He was right because he was simply quoting **Romans 8: 23-25.** We have hope in the Second Coming of Jesus. We have hope in the fact that the Spirit can make us to be more and more like God. We have hope because we know Jesus will never leave us or forsake us. "Love always hopes." What does this mean for you and me? Perhaps it means because of our love for others, because of our love for God, others will see our hope. "Those who hope in the Lord will renew their strength. They will soar on wings like eagles; they will run and not grow weary, they will walk and not be faint" (**Isaiah 40:31**). "In your hearts set apart Christ as Lord. Always be prepared to give an answer to everyone who asks you to give the reason for the hope that you have" (**1 Peter 3:15**). I wonder if perhaps it can be defined in the sharing of Jesus Christ—as the hope of everyone—with everyone?

PERSEVERANCE

This one is an easy one to type out. Love perseveres when: no one loves you back, everyone is impatient, unkind, envious, rude, boastful, proud, selfish, and angry with you. It perseveres on good and bad days. Until finally, finally, someone realizes they like it. Love always, always, perseveres, and with a perseverant love there will always be results.

LOVE NEVER FAILS

This one has already been covered under ACME LOVE. But stop for just a moment, and realize if love indeed never does fail, then all fifteen of the above descriptions of love must be in tact in your life. They must be practiced without favoritism. They must be lived without vacations because love will never, ever, not in a million years, fail. God is love and He is guaranteed for eternity! Praise Him! Praise Him! Praise Him!

We started FOUNDATIONS and CORNER-STONES a long time ago, but if you will put these things into practice you will find your life a lot more balanced. It will surprise you how often people come up to you ask for some of your time. Everyone wants to be loved, and when they find they can get it through you, they will be drawn to you. People were drawn to Jesus because He took the time to love them. I pray God will bless you as you seek to incorporate these things into your daily life. Please pray that God will continue to teach me about the FOUNDATIONS and CORNERSTONES found in 1 Corinthians 13.

CHAPTER FIVE

MY SISTER, MY BRIDE

Ihave struggled a little with where to include this section in the whole scheme of things. But I feel certain this is a good place for it. I think this is probably something people ought to know before they even begin looking into dating, romance, and ultimately, marriage. I initially wrote this with men in mind and have probably been guilty of writing this entire work with men in mind—after all, I am a man—but I am certain this has great ramifications for the women who read this as well. In fact, I encourage women to read this section so that they may know how their prospective husbands should treat them. That said, let us look at some verses.

"You have made my heat beat faster, **my sister, my bride**; you have made my heart beat faster with a single glance of your eyes, with a single strand of your necklace. How beautiful is your love, **my sister, my bride**! How much better is your love than wine, and the fragrance of your oils than all kinds of spices! Your lips, my bride, drip honey; honey and milk are under your tongue, and the fragrance of your garments is like the fragrance of Lebanon. A garden locked **is my sister, my bride**, a rock garden locked, a spring sealed up." **(Song of Solomon 4: 9-12)**

"I have come into my garden, **my sister, my bride**; I have gathered my myrrh along with my balsam. I have eaten my honeycomb and my honey; I have drunk my wine and my milk. Eat, friends; drink and imbibe deeply, o lovers. I was asleep but my heart was awake. A voice! My beloved was knocking; 'Open to me, **my sister, my bride**, my dove, my perfect one! For my head is drenched with dew, my locks with the damp of the night.'" **(Song of Solomon 5: 1-2)**

Look at these passages and you will notice something they hold in common (I made it easier for you by highlighting the text I wanted you to notice). "My sister, my bride." What does it mean? Why is it in the Bible five times in just ten verses? Why does Solomon use this phrase so much on his wedding night? What can we learn by it? Now, I have tried to be honest and a bit vulnerable throughout these notes. Perhaps that is not a completely good thing, but my thinking is that perhaps in my sin and shortcomings and, on rare occasion, the things I have done right,

I might better teach you by being a person you can identify with. That said, I recently fell into trouble when I ignored the obvious lesson of this phrase. I believe that "my sister, my bride" is written to be a guide for how things should be ordered in a relationship. I had been single for a long time. I had been praying for my wife almost daily and, in most cases, multiple times throughout the day. Every time I went on a road trip to preach I would think things like, "that is where my wife would sit" or, "this is when my wife would have prayed for me" or, "my wife would have talked to that girl." I began to miss her. Not the kind of miss you might think. It got to the point where I felt like I had her in my life and then lost her. It felt like the greatest love of my life had died and at this point I had not even met her. I missed her every day. It would not have been an unfair statement to say that I loved my wife for years prior to her coming. In fact, you could say of me that though I did not know her, I loved her. There is an old song with a line that says, "And though I don't know where you are, I know you must be there… and though I don't know who you are, I know you're beautiful." Well, that has been the case for me for the last several years; longing for and loving my bride. Recently I met someone and my heart was quickly knit to hers, but there was one problem. I could see her as my bride, but I didn't yet know her as my sister. I was so eager to have a bride and because she was the first one in five years to catch my eyes, I jumped to the place in my mind where she must be the fulfillment of all I had prayed for. Yet we never really became friends. I didn't know what it was to appreciate her as my sister in Christ. The result was that we fought a lot. She wanted a brother and a friend first then a husband and I was eager to skip the "sister" part and make her my bride. Yes, there is a reason for the order of things. Men, before you start thinking "bride" you should be thinking "sister". So many people these days (and, unfortunately, including myself) skip the "sister" stage and jump right into the "bride" stage. We forget to get to know the woman and never learn to love her as a woman, as an individual. We can see her as a bride and how she may fit into our lives, but we fail to see who she is, where her walk with God has gone, and where it will take her. I'm not saying that physical attraction shouldn't be there, or that you can't even think toward marriage, but your first thought should be "sister." This is vital for a couple of reasons. First, it is vital because you will grow to appreciate her more. Second, it is vital because it will keep you from defrauding her.

As I write this final edit and add this paragraph I have now been married for a year and a month. My wife, Michele, is a treasure to me. I have never had more fun or laughed more than I do with her. She is a delight to me. I admire so much about her and even though our courtship was a short one I looked at her first as my sister. Let me give you another example.

As I mentioned earlier, I have three sisters. Haley is almost three years younger than I am. As adults we get along pretty well; we didn't always get along as kids. In fact, you might as well know that as kids she was tougher than me and once even broke my nose when I was 15. But we have come a long way. In 1999 she got married and I gave her away; it was such a great moment in my life (I'll touch more on that in a moment). Now Haley lives with her husband, Brian, in a nice little house with their two boys, Camden and Jackson, and is expecting her third soon. Over the years I have really come to admire her. She is a good mother; she loves her boys and exhibits the utmost patience with them. She nurtures them, prays with them, and teaches them to pray and recite scripture. She serves with my brother-in-law at their church in the children's ministry and plays a huge role on Sunday mornings. On Sunday nights she teaches the seventh-grade class. When I was a kid, I never thought to admire her (plus, how many of us really admire the person who can break our nose?). I only came to admire her over time. We haven't always gotten along and we don't always see eye to eye, but she is my sister forever and that goes much deeper than just the blood in our veins. Hopefully, I will always be faithful to come to her defense and aide should she need me. Our friendship is built on something deeper now. When we pursue a "bride" rather than knowing a "sister," we miss an important part of the growth process that would make for a far superior marriage. It is harder to see your "bride" as your "sister" than it is to have your "sister" become your "bride."

The second reason it's important to see her as your sister first is so you might always honor her in the physical relationship. It is unfortunately a very easy thing to fall into physical misconduct. But only perverted men dishonor their sisters. When I gave my sister away at her wedding, the minister asked "who gives this woman to be joined to this man?" I answered, "Her mother and I do." I gave my sister away to be married to my brother-in-law. Think of the girl you are dating in that respect. You are just keeping her; your courtship with her is nothing more than walking her down the aisle to present her to her husband. If you are in the habit of dating many people, then you are responsible for many sisters. (Which, for the record, I do not encourage.) How have you honored them? We as men should guard our sisters fiercely. In Genesis 34, Dinah, the sister of the twelve sons of Israel, is raped; the rapist says he loves Dinah and wants to marry her. When the brothers find out, the Bible says, "the men were grieved, and they were very angry because he had done a disgraceful thing in Israel." Later, two of the brothers retaliated: "Now it came about on the third day, when they were in pain, that two of Jacob's sons, Simeon and Levi, Dinah's brothers, each took his sword and came upon the city unawares, and killed every male" (**Genesis 34:7, 25**). They were not content to have their sister defiled and do nothing about it. Wouldn't we do the same if someone harmed our sisters? Maybe you don't have a sister, but how would you respond if someone harmed your cousin, friend, mom, niece, or daughter? The Bible is not insulting women when it calls them the weaker vessel (**1 Peter 3:7**), but it is rather an indication that we should care tenderly for them. If I can view the woman I am dating as my sister first, then my inclination will always be to honor her. In the Bible it was acceptable to marry your half-sister. (Wow! I'm glad that isn't the case anymore!) There is a story of a prince named Amnon, one of David's sons, who is in love with his half-sister Tamar. Through deceit and trickery he gets her to come to his bedroom and "he took hold of her and said to her, 'come, lie with me, my sister'" (**2 Samuel 13:11**). Now this may sound gross to us, but as half-siblings they could have been married. Tamar entreats Amnon not to violate her and even says, "Please speak to the king, for he will not withhold me from you" (**2 Samuel 13:13**). She was willing to marry her half-brother. Amnon won't hear of it and "since he was stronger than she, he violated her and lay with her" (**2 Samuel 13:14**). "Then Amnon hated her with a very great hatred; for the hatred with which he hated her was greater than the love with which he had loved her. And Amnon said to her, 'Get up, go away!'" (**2 Samuel 13:15**). He took advantage of his sister and ultimately hated her more than he had ever loved her. Absalom, the full brother of Tamar, learns of Amnon's treachery, lies in wait for two years, and eventually has Amnon put to death.

We need to be the kind of men who will treat the women around us like full flesh-and-blood sisters. We need to be men who honor women at all costs and treat them with tenderness and grace. A good friend of mine and I were discussing this particular section of the Love Notes when he said he finds his sisters beautiful but has never looked at his sister and said, "man, now she IS SO fine!" That would be disturbing. In fact, he went on to say he only found his sisters beautiful as he matured and was able to see them as women. When we are kids we don't really consider beauty very much, do we? Our friends become beautiful to us because we have come to know them and love them. Let us not defraud our sisters in Christ by not loving them as sisters first, and after that, as brides. *Let me add that though I always found Michele beautiful I consistently find myself more and more attracted to her. And so it will always be. *

It is also relevant to ponder the question, "Why does Solomon use this phrase so liberally on his wedding night as he is standing there naked with his bride and as he consummates the marriage through sexual intercourse?" I can only tell you what I think. It is my opinion (ladies, please correct me if I am wrong) that while women want their husbands to be sexually attracted to them, and while they want their husbands to find them desirable, women also want to know that they are admired and respected. Women want to know that their thoughts and opinions matter and that their achievements are at least worthy of notoriety and praise to their husbands. When a man will come to his bride and declare, "My sister, my bride," he is noting all those things that make her unique apart from him, and he is noting all those things that make her unique together with him. We men need to learn to praise and acknowledge the "sister" part of our bride, so that we may fully enjoy our bride, but also that we may fully bless her.

Long for a bride, pray for her, weep for her, yearn for her, but find her in a sister.

CHAPTER SIX

IF DATING ISN'T IN THE BIBLE HOW DO I DO IT?

Dating isn't in the Bible. Pious people these days stare down their noses at you and say "God's way isn't dating that is why I follow the biblical patterns of courtship." I can't stand it when people say that. That's not to say that courtship doesn't have good safeguards for the young couple but the truth is that the Bible doesn't even mention courtship. In fact the biblical method for finding a spouse is arranged marriages. We don't tend to do that much in our culture, but we do tend to date. So let us move on and briefly cover three principles of dating that must be carried over to our married lives.

1. God must be the center of the relationship. Now I imagine you are nodding your head in agreement. If you have been in the church at all lately and are dating-eligible, you have been told how important

it is to have God at the center of your relationship. I am sure from time to time you have been given a list of things to put into your relationship to make it God centered, but it is not that list we look to. Praying, going to church together, studying the Bible together…these things are good, but not the litmus paper of a God-centered relationship. (In fact these things don't even necessarily mean that you are saved.) The true measure of a relationship focused on God comes after the date, or after the phone call. Women, if after the date you find yourself wanting to know God better because of the guy you were with, and men, if after the date you find yourself wanting to know God better because of the girl you were with, then you have a God-centered relationship. That's it! It cannot be one sided; if I'm dating someone and talking to her makes me want to know God better, but I am aware that she does not desire to know Him more when she is with me, then our relationship is not where it is supposed to be. If you are in a relationship that is not God-centered you need to get out now! Do not tell yourself that you are going to change the other person. If you are coming away from the relationship without seeing God better, that relationship is not worth your time. I heard someone once say, "Men, when you are looking for a wife, find one that will out-pray you." I would take that further and say, women, when you are looking for a husband, find one that will out-pray you. Get involved in a relationship that thrusts you into the lap of God and encourages your prayer and study time, or do not get involved in one at all!

2. Every physical thing must be other-centered. This is going to be something perhaps you won't like to hear, but it's something I think is vital in a Godly dating relationship. Today one of the big questions is, "How far is too far?" What exactly can we do in a relationship without crossing any boundaries? Even asking that question is probably out of line. After all, when we ask what is out of bounds, don't we do so with the intention of getting as close to the edge as possible without going over? The bad thing about edges is that very often they are undercut. Sometimes on the edge of a river the water has washed away a lot of dirt you cannot see; as you step up to the edge your weight causes you to plummet right into the frigid water. We cannot be prepared for it. How close would you be willing to get to quicksand before becoming afraid of sinking to the bottom? Almost all of us think we can handle the pressures of a physical relationship; we want to be able to handle it. Yet it seems so often we start the physical relationship and it runs out of control, across lines we thought were firmly established. Guilt sweeps over us and we cringe when sexual immorality is mentioned in the Bible or in a church service. In the Old Testament you would set up boundary stones to mark your property. If you moved someone else's boundary stone to encroach on their land, you could be put to death.

I would recommend that you set up boundary stones before the relationship even really gets started. Then never ever cross them. What I want to do is change the way you look at the physical relationship, and by doing so, hopefully prevent you from "crossing any more lines." When you enter into a physical relationship you most often end up defrauding the person you're dating. You will find a better explanation of this under the heading "An Adulterous Relationship."

First, it is important to remember that love is not self-seeking (I told you we would come back to it). Now, it has been a long time since I held anyone's hand, and even longer since I have kissed anyone, but if my memory is worth anything, I think I liked it. But I have learned I cannot hold someone's hand or kiss someone because I like the way it makes me feel. If I was on a date with someone and it had been two years since I had kissed anyone, I may want to try that again. If I do it because I want to receive pleasure from it—because I want to feel nice—then it is wrong. I will take it a step further and say it is sin. Please, do not misunderstand me; it is not wrong to enjoy a kiss. The wife of Solomon loved to be kissed by him and he loved the way she looked. It is alright to enjoy kissing and holding hands. Love the right way gives you joy and pleasure; in fact, it glorifies God when we honor Him with this part of our relationship. The Bible says to delight in your wife; our wives were, at some point, our fiancées, and, at some other point, our girlfriends, so we can delight in our girlfriends as well. Because you love her, or because you love him, and because you delight in him or her, you will want to kiss and hold hands. However, if your physical activity is prompted out of a desire for pleasure, then it is wrong, because it has become selfish. I can say that because we already know that love IS NOT self-seeking. Love itself will reward you! If you are doing physical things in the relationship for your own benefit, you are seeking your own pleasure. That is not character-istic of love. Rather, holding hands, kissing, and one day in a marriage relationship, sex, should be prompted out of the love you have for the other individual. Guys, you should want to hold her hand as a way of saying, "hey, I'm here for you." The kiss should tell her that you care very much for her, not that you have no control of yourself. And you know, as you learn to hold hands the right way, and to kiss the right way, you'll find, I believe, that you enjoy it more than the selfish physical contact. Again, if you are doing it for yourself it is sin!

Second, keep your physical relationship in control by giving it over to God. Since the summer of 1995, a prayer of accountability has preceded every date I have had. I pray out loud—in front of both the girl and God—that God would teach me to honor and respect her as he does. I pray that God would show me how to love her as he does so that even my thoughts would not be displeasing to Him. Then the date begins. I can tell you that every time I have prayed that prayer, I have been completely pure in body and mind. To the same measure, and sad to say, when I have failed to pray that prayer I have found myself often in trouble, either with thought or situations. I would also suggest that after the first kiss you stop, and ask God to guard your hearts. I have found that once the kissing starts, moral tendencies begin to slide. Honor God in the physical part of your relationship. I put the main weight of physical purity upon the man in the relationship. As the man, it is imperative that you be responsible in the relationship for the physical purity of things. We are instructed in the bible to treat "the older women as mothers and the younger women as sisters in all purity" (**1 Timothy 5:2**). Since everyone you ever date will be either older or younger than you, this may be a helpful verse to learn. You will notice it says to treat these younger women in all purity. Later, we will look in more depth into the importance of sexual purity in the relationship.

If today you are in a relationship and you realize you are holding hands or kissing for selfish reasons, I challenge you to set that aside and wait until God gives you the go-ahead. It may be hard to quit kissing now, but later when you can look back and say that the relationship has honored God, you will rejoice.

3. Finally, you must learn what it means to love the right way. I know if you stopped reading after just

that first sentence you would have the tendency to say, "I thought that is what I was doing." But remember, we only covered Foundations and Cornerstones. There is so much more to it than that. I suggest that you take dating a lot more seriously. Did you know there is no reference to dating in the Bible? But since today we use dating to find our husband or wife, I think we need to put more importance on it than we have. I will not date someone I know I would not marry. In fact if you can't get married now then you really shouldn't be dating. I will not have a second date with someone if on the first date I realize they are not what I need in a spouse. (i.e. if they are ungodly in some obvious way) Still, so many of us date just to date; we do it for entertainment and fun. Yes, dating is supposed to be both fun and entertaining, but it is much more important than that. I do not know what you ladies have been told over the years. I would be willing to bet that most guys have heard someone say, "You need to treat the woman you are dating like you want your wife to be treated by the guy she is dating right now." Wow! That should step up the way we date. What I want you to begin thinking about is this: what if the person dating your wife or your husband right now is you? Just in case, you had better love them the right way. If you do not end up married to the one you are dating, it is important for you to have loved them rightly. Really, this section is going to be carried over to the marriage part. Stick with me, because there is still so much to learn.

CHAPTER SEVEN

AN ADULTEROUS RELATIONSHIP

3-20-03
My One Love,

I want you to know that not only will I never engage in a physical adulterous relationship, I pledge that I will keep my looks of longing for you alone. You alone will turn my head. You alone will stir up thoughts of intimacy. You alone I will delight in. You alone will I long for when I am apart from you. Please know that my heart, my mind, my eyes, and my body will be reserved for you and for you alone. I love you still not knowing you.

ryan

Most of us despise the idea of adultery. In fact, almost all people, Christian and Non-Christian alike, agree that adultery is flat out wrong. More than that, most of these people believe that adultery is not just sexual intercourse with someone other than your spouse. In fact, some people, again both Christian and those who are not, would say that going to lunch often, or spending a lot of time alone with a person of the opposite sex, is adultery. That may be hard for you to hear; perhaps if you are single you think you do not have to worry about adultery at all right now. Let us take the definition of adultery a bit farther and see what Christ has to say about it. "You have heard it said, do not commit adultery. But I tell you that anyone who looks at a woman lustfully has already committed adultery with her in his heart" (**Matthew 5: 27, 28**). This may be a tough pill to swallow but what Christ is saying is if you look wantingly, powerfully, or lustfully after someone, you have committed adultery. This is true for the married person reading this and the single person. Every time you look lustfully at a woman's body several things happen. One is that your mind becomes filled with sexual desires. The only time that sexual desires bring glory to God is when they are contained within the confines of marriage. Second, you have successfully cheated on your spouse whether you already have one or are waiting for one. Finally, you have defrauded the individual whom you have sought lustfully. Let me explain what I mean. Look at the first eight verses of **1 Thessalonians chapter 4**.

> "Finally then, brethren, we urge and exhort in the Lord Jesus that you should abound more and more, just as you received from us

how you ought to walk and to please God; for you know what commandments we gave you through the Lord Jesus. For this is the will of God, your sanctification: that you should abstain from sexual immorality; that each of you should know how to possess his own vessel in sanctification and honor, not in passion of lust, like the Gentiles who do not know God; that no one should take advantage of and defraud his brother in this matter, because the Lord is the avenger of all such, as we also forewarned you and testified. For God did not call us to uncleanness, but in holiness. Therefore he who rejects this does not reject man, but God, who has given us His Holy Spirit."

Why I have not noticed this before, I'm really not sure. But when we do not control our bodies we cheat and defraud our brother or sister. Take note of the above passage. God will visit us for doing so, and it will not be good. Having looked at what Christ says in **Matthew 5** we can defraud our brother or sister even in our hearts. If we defraud someone in our hearts, they are not in sin because they have played no part, but we ourselves have still taken advantage of them on some level. To whatever extent we go with someone physically, we have stolen from him or her, their future spouse, our future spouse and even ourselves. It is not for me to make out with someone who will belong to another man, nor do I want someone to make out with the one who will be my wife. When I pursue my physical lusts I am robbing myself of the pleasure of knowing my wife alone in this manner. I am stealing from this woman I won't marry that which only her husband should have done for her or to her. I am robbing my future wife of the joy of knowing that I have loved her alone physically and I am a thief by taking what belongs to another man. Perhaps then, we should refrain from all romantic relationally based physical contact unless we are certain that the person before us is our bride or our groom. Even if we are certain we are going to marry the person we have to be careful that we are honoring them as Christ would have us do. And most certainly we should refrain from all that would cheat someone or steal the blessing of the joy of marriage. This is a hard teaching. I regret I did not learn this much earlier, so as to protect myself from ill-gotten situations and sinful lusts.

CHAPTER EIGHT

TRUTHS ABOUT THE BRIDE

FIRST, THE BRIDE OF CHRIST

I cannot teach you the joy found in being the bride of Christ. But I can tell you that you will know no greater joy, will not be more filled or fulfilled, pleased or satisfied, you will not obtain the best-ever marriage relationship until you first understand your role and relationship as the bride of Christ. When in joyous worship you fall down on your face before God almighty, when you awake with scripture or praise songs already on your tongue, when you are moved to tears because of the incredible love God has for you and has demonstrated to you, then you have but a taste of understanding. You have but a breath of the life that is in your husband, Christ, and the joy found in Him. When you have looked to all of His creation and all of His work and have searched it out and fathomed the depth of it all, then you have only touched the hem of His ways. (**Job 26:7-14**)

One thing that will help you as you consider being the bride of Christ is to remember that our marriage relationship to Him is not patterned after earthly relationships, but earthly marriage is to be patterned after our marriage to Christ; if we do not relate well to our husband Christ, we will not do well in our earthly marriage. The most intimate thing in an earthly marriage is the sexual relationship designed by God for a man and his wife to share. If in fact our earthly marriage is patterned after our marriage to God, what is the most intimate way we can relate to Him? We are soon going to look at Song of Solomon and see on the wedding night how the Husband admires his wife's body but does not engage her sexually until she invites him to do so. It is important to note that at this point the couple is already married. What is the significance of this to us, as it relates to being the bride of Christ? First, we agree that to be the bride of Christ—to be married to Him—we must belong to Him. In other words, we are Christians. But just as it is true in Song of Solomon, it is true in our marriage to Christ that He, despite being our husband, will not take from us our most intimate part until we offer it to Him. I confess I do not exactly know what that means and I do not think I can give a broad generalized answer. What I do know is that God desires to relate to us in a more intimate manner than simply being our husband. It is true in an earthly marriage that people don't get married never to desire or experience the physical intimacy found in a sexual relationship. Imagine a man in love with a woman, pledging himself to her and vice-versa, and upon the conclusion of their marriage vows she says, "now I don't want you to ever touch me intimately. I simply want you to be my husband." We would identify that there is a problem and that the marriage is not going to thrive. In the same way, when we become the brides of Christ, and He becomes our husband, if we do not give the most intimate parts of ourselves to Him the marriage is not going to thrive. Whatever is dear to you, whatever is most precious to you, it is that which you must give your husband who is called Jesus, before you will ever be able to under-stand what it means to be His bride; if not, you will never fully take hold of what His plan is for you in an earthly, God-ordained marriage. I understand that you may feel confused as I speak in one moment of being married in an earthly relationship and in the next moment speak of being married to Christ but I want you to know again that until we understand that God is the pattern for all that we could learn of love, we will never love rightly. Our relationships will fail, our marriages will fail (as they are already doing at a rate of 54%) until we come to understand the love that comes from and through God.

THE BLESSING OF A BRIDE

Every day of my life these days (these days being summer 2004 and 29 years old), I pray my life may be blessed by a bride. My bride! The woman in white who will come through the doors, steal away my breath, and fade from my vision as my eyes are flooded with tears. Every day I pray for the scent of her hair to fill my nostrils and for her hand to fill my own. Some of you reading this are convinced I'm brainwashed—or at best deceived or naïve—to believe my bride would be such a blessing in my life. You contemplate the fights or the prospective disagreements. You recollect the shouting and slamming doors that plagued your parent's home; you recall with bitterness the nights on the couch or the cold icy words that greeted you when you came home. True, these things have invaded marriages, but I am not naïve to expect better; nor am I deceived, for the Bible teaches clearly what marriage ought to be and I have contented myself with nothing less than the teachings of Scripture. So every day I expect the blessing and not the heartache, the joy and not the pain, the love and none of the disdain. God has designed the wife to be the chief of blessings to the husband. "Your wife shall be like a fruitful vine, within your house, your children like olive plants around your table. Behold, for **thus shall the man be blessed** who fears the LORD" (**Psalm 128: 3,4** NAS emphasis mine). And again, "Enjoy life with the woman whom you love all the days of your fleeting life which [God] has given to you under the sun; for **this is your reward in life**, and in your toil in which you have labored under the sun" (**Ecclesiastes 9:9** NAS emphasis mine). How many times I have cried out to God "I fear you! With all of my heart I fear you! Where is my 'fruitful vine?' Where is my wife, my blessing?" As of yet there is nothing but silence. Still, I will not lose sight of the fact that my wife is to be my blessing. She is my "fruitful vine," my nurturing, my food, my sustenance. And what does the Bible tell us in Ecclesiastes? "Enjoy life with the woman you love... for this is your reward in life." No wonder so many marriages are in ruins and devastation, they failed to note the union as a blessing and as a reward. It may have been an informed decision; it may have "just seemed like it was time." Or it may have been "the right thing to do." But it should have been THE blessing, THE reward! How many of you have been foolish married folk and have forsaken the enjoying? Husbands, "enjoy life with the woman you love!" This isn't about sex or her not arguing with you about who is going to bathe the kids. This is enjoyment. This is a jovial laugh at silly circumstances, the scream of delight as the roller coaster plummets and hair flies, silence and wonder shared as the sun falls into the deep blue ocean, the scent of one another on your clothes after a nap on the couch. Enjoy her! Watch her today as she moves through the house. Remember when you saw her as delicate? Remember when you enjoyed life with her? Enjoy her once more! She is your blessing! She is your reward! She is the height of all you will ever have in your life! No blessing can match her! No endeavor is worth more time spent! No investment will ever reap higher dividends! Enjoy her! Kiss her again like the first time. Hold her like she would be lost if you didn't. Speak to her like tender words are her only breath. Enjoy her! Ecclesiastes tells us that enjoying our wife is the very thing we have labored for under the sun. All that your life was spent for is in her, the woman sleeping next to you, fixing the macaroni and cheese for the kids, crying at loss, laughing at joy, sharing your day. It is all for her. Enjoy her! And again I say enjoy her! She is the blessing of God in your life; what a wonderful blessing she is. * In the 20 months that I have known and been married to Michele I can say honestly that we have not had one fight nor have we raised voices or slammed doors. We have enjoyed one another. We have laughed. Sure, I have said stupid things and hurt her feelings but I have always been immediate to get things right. Everything that I have so long prayed for, looked for, and prepared for I have found. It isn't about being idealistic. It is about building a marriage after the outline given to us in scripture, and doing so long before the marriage ever starts and way before the girl is even a blip on the radar. When we obey the word of God we find that it is right. What a blessing it all is! How I enjoy my wife! *

Wives, be certain that in all your doings you are showing yourself forth as the highest blessing of God in your husband's life. Whatever else may be his blessing, be certain you are the highest one; act accordingly. You are a fruitful vine. Be careful your fruit is still sweet and your vine has not withered in bitterness. Provide shade for his head when things are hard and fruit for his body when he is weary. Be his oasis, his reward. How confused it must make a man to have his greatest blessing most resemble a thorny hedge. No wonder he focuses on the smaller blessings of job, money, fame, and recognition. You are the height of all he will ever know; does your daily life reflect this? We will look more later at what it means to be a wife of noble character but for now keep in mind that God tells the husband that the wife is his highest blessing. Don't settle for being less than that. Seek out ways to be a blessing to your husband.

7-15-04
My Beloved,

What a great blessing you must be! Days seem long without you, but I seek my God and fear Him and I shall be blessed! I love you and long for you. Come, Blessing, Come! May I see your face and hear your voice. I love you.

ryan

CHAPTER NINE

BETTER TWO THAN ONE, BETTER ONE THAN TWO

Don't let the title fool you; this is not a contradiction in terms. At least it isn't once we've defined the terms. Let us begin with the first part. The Bible says,

> "Two are better than one because they have a good return for their labor. For if either of them falls, the one will lift up his companion. But woe to the one who falls when there is not another to lift him up. Furthermore, if two lie down together they keep warm, but how can one be warm alone? And if one can overpower him who is alone, two can resist him. A cord of three strands is not quickly torn apart." (**Ecclesiastes 4:9-12** NAS)

So we see that two are better than one. This passage is used in many weddings and I think rightly so. This is a great picture of some of the blessing that comes through the marriage union.

Two "have a good return for their labor." Unfortunately, this is not always true in our marriages today. The exception to this statement is when the two are not working together but, rather, on two different jobs. Fortunately for us, the text is teaching these two are laboring together in like-minded devotion to their task. When two come together for a common labor, they will have a great return for their work—accomplishing more than could be done individually. This is true for several reasons. One, because basic math teaches that four is more than two; if you have four hands, then in theory they are able to do twice the amount. Second, when we labor with someone and one begins to slow the pace, the other is there to encourage the finishing of the labor. You will notice the text says if one of the laborers falls, the other there to pick up again is. Unfortunately, in many marriages today when one falls, the other laborer criticizes and judges, rather than lifts up the fallen worker. We spend so much time focusing on faults and shortcomings, that at the end of the day the labor is left largely undone; it shall be the same tomorrow and the next day and the next for twenty years until the laborers find themselves harboring resentment and bitterness. The marriage relationship should be looked at as two laborers working on the same job. So often we compartmentalize what the husband or wife is supposed to do; one thinks the labor of the other is beneath them, or not their responsibility, so it gets overlooked. When the couple will come together to labor for all things under their roof as one, the labor will be accomplished, rewarding, and surprisingly sweeter than the labor done alone. Strive to labor together; it is not about "his work" or "her work." You're married, so now it is about "our work."

Two can "keep warm." In my ministry, I travel, work with, and meet many couples. I have had many chances to be a guest in their homes. Some are very kind and gracious to one another yet many of them seem cold to one another; scarcely touching or even looking at one another. They give each other formal and forced niceties in public yet seem distant from one another in their homes. A rough hello and he is off to read the paper after work. A muffled goodnight and she slips off to bed; they keep waiting for the other to show tenderness or interest once again. They have forgotten they are the blanket, so to speak. So often we find ourselves so worried about how cold we are in the house that we forget that we are to warm up the other. Quit focusing on how cold you are in your house, how lonely, or how deprived, and be the blanket of warmth for your spouse. When two lie down together they keep warm. No wonder your home seems cold, the last time you laid down together was... was...can you remember? I'm not talking about actually laying down together side by side (though that may be needed as well), but rather I'm talking about being the warmth the other person requires. Anyone can freeze to death; perhaps your relationship has you on the brink of freezing. Instead of worrying so much about how you might keep warm, consider how you might warm the other. Be warm to one another and see if things don't change in your household. As long as you lie down by yourself, as long as you think of yourself alone—your needs alone—as long as you are selfish and self-seeking, you will be cold. Come together again; lay together again, and be warm. * I had been married for six months when my wife and I were at a youth camp where I was preaching. It had been a very difficult day resulting in many people being unhappy with me and I was discouraged and questioning my ministry. I went back to my hotel room before dinner to look over my notes for the evening sermon and to get a shower. But I couldn't seem do anything but lay in bed with the lights off. As I lay there, my wife came and lay down next to me and gave me a hug, and then she just began to pray for me. As she prayed she cried. She asked God to give me peace. She asked God to comfort me. She asked God to make me confident in the things I was teaching. She comforted me and kept me warm and strengthened me for the task at hand. That night I really understood what Ecclesiastes meant. *

Two can "resist him." Whoever "him" may be and whenever he shows up, know for certain that alone you are likely to perish. But together you will be a force and strong arm of defense, a bulwark. There will be plenty of "hims" in your life, in your marriage; be certain you do not face "him" alone. Seek the help, the strength, of the other. Together you will be victorious. Too many people in marriage face their fears, their concerns, their doubts, and their "hims" alone, unwilling to tell their spouse. I think this stems from a neglect of the first two points. If the couple would labor together and keep one another warm, they would also war against "him" together. But when one spouse feels they are working in the marriage alone, and the other feels cold, it is only natural to face their problems alone. Marriages are being destroyed. Resist together, war together, against the "hims" in your life. You will overpower "him" together.

So then we see that two are in fact better than one, but what about the "Better one than two" that I put at the heading of this section? Well, the Bible teaches that when we get married we become "one flesh." It is better to be married than alone (that is "better two than one"), but when you are married you are to think of yourself as one in the marriage and not two (thus the "better one than two"). May God richly bless your labor, your warmth, and your resisting as you come together. Let's look more at what it means to be one flesh.

CHAPTER TEN

LEAVE AND CLEAVE: BECOMING ONE FLESH

"For this cause (reason) a man shall leave his father and his mother, and shall cleave to his wife and they shall become one flesh" (**Genesis 2:24** NAS). Wait, for what reason? I want to know the reason! Remember when you were a child and your parents and their adult friends would say something about you and chuckle a little bit? They weren't making fun or ridiculing (though at times they may have been), they simply were observing a cute little kid. But you say, "Tell me. What's so funny? Mommmmm. Tell me!" Well, I get the same feeling when I read this verse. What's the reason again? Ok, sure, I can see the leaving his father and mother part; there comes a time when someone must grow up...but the cleave part? What was the reason for that? Wilson's Old Testament Word Studies says that cleave in this verse means these things: "to stick, as things that are glued together, as clods of earth, to be closely joined together, as the scales and flakes of Leviathan mentioned in Job. To adhere to, to follow hard after..." And the list goes on and on. So again I cry out, "God, what is the reason I should leave, cleave, and become one flesh?!" There are, I think, three reasons contained in the preceding verses.

First, "'it is not good for the man to be alone...'" (**Genesis 2:18**). Man, alone? Sure, Adam was alone, but every man thereafter has companionship, don't they? Was God speaking of Adam only when He said this? No way! Remember "for this reason a man shall leave his father and mother." When God spoke these words He spoke them throughout eternity. The alone here is not absence of companionship; in the sovereignty of God—as His eyes gazed at the looming future, as His heart felt the very heart of mankind—God knew it was not good for man to be alone, to be absent of that one whom he can cleave to. Another image of the word cleave is the image of a man cleaving to the ground as he prostrates himself before God. God knew the absence of this opportunity to cleave to someone was not beneficial to man. We do not cleave to our friends, obviously, not nearly like we have the opportunity to in a marriage relationship. So the first reason we leave, cleave, and become one is because God saw it was not good without this. Does that mean all men should marry? No. We will find later that some (very few) have the gift, ability, and privilege to be single throughout their days on earth.

Second, "'I will make a helper suitable for him'" (**Genesis 2:18**). God has done this for us! He has made a helper suitable for every man He has appointed to be married. And every woman who has been appointed for marriage is one who was fashioned specifically by God to be a suitable helper, which is the greatest responsibility and blessing the wife will have. How fantastic is that?! Would we choose at any point not to enter into a blessing that God has so readily bestowed upon us (which we do daily, by the way)? So the reason given for leaving, cleaving, and being one comes down to the fact that God has done this for us! For our benefit! How wonderful!

Finally, "and the man said, 'this is now bone of my bones, and flesh of my flesh; she shall be called woman, because she was taken out of man'" (**Genesis 2:23**). Woman was brought forth from man for him. If from one man (Adam) all enter into sin, and if through one man (Christ) all may be freed from sin, then because woman was taken once from man to be fashioned for him she is perpetually taken from man. Men, there is someone, somewhere, considering you are to be married, who was formed from you, for you. Equally, you are for her. Ladies, there is someone, somewhere, considering you are to be married, who you were formed from and for. Equally, he is for you.

So then, "this reason," "this cause," is because God saw it was good for man to have the opportunity to cleave, because He created us for it, and because men and women are from each other (**1 Corinthians 11:11-12**). Here then is the cause.

Now, be certain you do not leave out any of the three components of marriage. Be sure you leave, cleave, and become one flesh. The "one flesh" part most people seem to understand; call it instinct or something. Let us look at "leave" first. If your parents were beneficial to you in your growing up years, the tendency may be to lean too heavily on them in marriage. Rather, you are to "leave" mother and father. This is more than just in body; it means your parents aren't telling you what house to buy, when to have kids, what job to take, or what extra-curricular activities you are to be involved in. It is ok to seek your parent's counsel if they are godly and wise-minded; however, it would be better to seek the counsel of someone less biased, with more freedom to give advice based on scripture—not of personal preference for their son or daughter. If your parents were harmful to you in your growing years, you may find that a lot of mental briars remain. These briars, if you will allow my literary metaphor, will tangle and defeat your ability to communicate with your spouse. All of the insecurities birthed in you must be put aside, or at least be in a place where you are capable of dealing with them adequately. So often, my tendency in my insecurities is to glaze them over. That works fine for a moment, though it is not best. Eventually all will fail. So, whether they were a good or bad influence in your life, be sure you leave your mother and father. This is not their marriage; it is yours. It is your marriage before God, not before your family. It is your marriage that must be according to God's plan, not your parents. It is your marriage that must be holy, pure, and right before God, by Jesus, through the Spirit, not before parents, by dad through mom. That will destroy you. LEAVE!

Then cleave! Join yourself tightly to your spouse. This is not so much a sexual thing as it is an all-encompassing thing. Be tightly knit together; come together in one Spirit, and one mind in Christ. Make it as hard to distinguish you as two people as it is to tell the difference between the oxygen and carbon dioxide floating around in our atmosphere. Resolve to be united under God's authority, not merely before Him. Ask your Father in heaven to show you what it means to be bound together. It is imperative that you cleave. "Leaving" is beneficial, but without cleaving, you don't have a marriage. You have a friendship of sorts, a partnership perhaps, but you do not have what it will take to make your marriage all it is to be in God. So CLEAVE and be one flesh! This same word is used in our relationship to God. In Deuteronomy we find that we are commanded to "fear the LORD your God; you shall serve Him and cleave to Him, and you shall swear by His name." (**Deuteronomy 10:20**) This was also the commitment that Ruth made to her mother-in-law in the book of Ruth. (**Ruth 1:14-18**) What we should learn is that cleaving is a covenant type decision. It is something we are dedicated and committed to. When we cleave to our spouse we are making a covenant before God that we will always be joined to them. You may not always feel the infat-uation that was there in the initial stages of your rela-tionship, but then we know that love isn't based on feelings. So cleave! When you cleave, stay there! If it is something that can be easily undone, then it wasn't cleaving to begin with.

SO NOW YOU'RE ONE FLESH

Remember, the Lord has made you one. Remember, in flesh and in spirit you are His. Why did God make you one? God did this so He might have godly offspring (**Malachi 2:15**). It will be your job as one to remember Christ with your life, so that your children will come to know Him in His fullness. Meanwhile, as you are married and not yet having children, please consider what it could mean for you to have godly offspring. As long as you do not have children of your own, could it be that you, as one flesh, are to produce godly offspring of those you have the opportunity to minister to and before? You can produce godly offspring that is not the fruit of your own womb.

It is hard to teach what it means to be one flesh, but let me remind you that you are to be tightly knit together; let me also remind you that you as a Christian couple are also joint heirs to all that Christ is heir to. Therefore, in the eternal scheme of things there is no separation between the two of you.

"For as many as are led by the Spirit of God, these are sons of God. For you did not receive the spirit of bondage again to fear, but you received the of adoption by whom we cry out, 'Abba, Father.' The Spirit Himself bears witness with our spirit that we are children of God, and if children, then heirs—heirs of

God and joint heirs with Christ, if indeed we suffer with Him, that we may also be glorified together." (**Romans 8:14-17**)

What joy it should bring you to be married and one with a fellow child of God, and heir to all the things of God. This knowledge in itself should keep you from ever perceiving yourself as above your spouse.

Another great reason to be joined as one flesh is found in **Ecclesiastes 4:9-12**. We looked at this a little already but let us study it a bit further.

"Two are better than one, because they have a good return for their work: if one falls down, his friend can help him up. But pity the man who falls and has no one to help him up. Also, if two lie down together, they will keep warm. But how can one keep warm alone? Though one may be overpowered, two can defend themselves. A cord of three strands is not quickly broken." (**Ecclesiastes 4: 9-12**)

If your arm aches, your whole body is aware of it. I once broke my toe; it was excruciatingly painful and though the pain was confined to my toe, my entire body knew about it. Occasionally you will meet someone who has a nerve disorder; they can cut a finger or toe without ever being aware of it. This will destroy a person's body given time. Now think of this in terms of a marriage being described as one flesh. You should be so close to one another that nothing hurts one without hurting the other. Further, if you hurt your body—if you gash it—don't you tend to it? Don't you dress the wound and treat it so it will heal? If one of you hurts, it is the obligation of the other not only to be aware of it, but also to be so concerned about it that you rush to mend the wound. Who, with a gaping hole in their leg casually thinks to themselves, "I'll get around to doing something about that later"? I was playing full-contact football with some friends of mine a number of years ago. One guy put a block on me that thrust his bald head into my chin. The next thing I knew I was laying on the ground with blood all over my shirt and a ringing in my ears. I told my roommates that I was going to sit out a play or two and then I'd come back in but they quickly let me know that my chin was in bad shape and needed stitches. Not believing them I told them I would walk across the street to the apartment and check out my situation and then be right back. However, when I got home I realized that my chin was in such bad shape that I could put my entire thumb in the gash. I immediately went to get stitches. But what if I had ignored the warnings of my friends? Or what if when I had seen it for myself I thought "oh, I'm sure it will take care of itself"? With that attitude one will fester, become infected, diseased, and then die. So it is true in our marriages. When we see problems and hurts and pains we should, in our marriage relationship as one flesh, leap upon our wounds with diligent attention and mend that which is broken, bind it up, and stitch what is torn, so it might once again come together. So many marriages fall to pieces due to the lack of interest in dressing the wounds of the "one flesh." In a like manner, when one part of the body is honored, are not all honored? Granted, if you put a $3,000.00 engagement ring on the finger of a woman, it is the finger that gets all the praise. Yet, does the body envy the finger or rejoice with it? I would suppose (having never been proposed to myself) that the entire body rejoices. * My wife has had her diamond now for about a year and a half and she will still wiggle her fingers in my face and say in a sweet little voice "so this is my diamond". Though the ring is only on her finger she finds that she still enjoys it in her whole person. * So when you are one flesh, and your spouse is exalted by man, text, position, education, or whatever it may be, you should rejoice that one part of your flesh has been lifted up for a time. To understand what it means to be bound together in this way will benefit your marriage inexplicably. May God Himself give you greater understanding than I can put in simple words here.

CHAPTER ELEVEN

WHAT GOD HAS JOINED TOGETHER

4-14-03

My Beloved,

God has joined us together; let us never seek to be put apart. Let us commit one to the other that "divorce" will never enter our vocabulary and never pierce our minds for a moment. God has brought us together and we will seek Him and He will hold us together. I love you forever.

ryan

When it comes to divorce, I must admit for a great deal of my life my position has been one that tended toward unforgiveness. God has taught me, however, that I must be as forgiving of this sin as any other. Divorce is a very harmful sin in our lives, but I think most often we don't view it as sin. However, **divorce**

has destroyed our lives, our expectation, our hope, our trust, our lives with God, our families, our futures, and has taught us that marriage is not permanent. How sad it is that people view divorce as a way out. I once heard of a pastor who spent an entire Sunday morning service on why divorce was alright; how that grieves my heart. We should never view divorce as a way out of something we don't like. If we are married, we have made a choice to be and, like any other commitment we make, we must work hard at it. We need to understand divorce is never pleasing to God. Sin is anything contrary to God's will; divorce is clearly against God's will, therefore it is sin. Do not for a moment believe that God is pleased with divorce. Clearly the Bible indicates that for marital infidelity, divorce is allowed, but Christ is quick to point out this is not how God intended it (**Matthew 19: 9, Matthew 5:32**).

"And some Pharisees came to Him, testing Him, and saying, 'Is it lawful for a man to divorce his wife for any cause at all?' And He answered and said, 'Have you not read, that He who created them from the beginning made them male and female, and said, 'For this cause a man shall leave his father and mother, and shall cleave to his wife; and the two shall become one flesh'? Consequently they are no longer two, but one flesh. *What therefore God has joined together, let no man separate.*' They said to Him, 'Why then did Moses command to give her a certificate of divorce and send her away?' He said to them, '*Because of your hardness of heart*, Moses permitted you to divorce your wives; *but from the beginning it has not been this way*.'" (**Matthew 19:3-8** NAS emphasis added)

Notice it says, "From the beginning it has not been this way." There is no beginning but that which comes from God. "What God has joined together, let no man separate." This passage should enable us to see that God does not delight in divorce. One other text I would like to share with you: "'Take heed then, to your spirit, and let no one deal treacherously against the wife of your youth. For *I hate divorce*,' *says the Lord*, *the God of Israel*, 'and him who covers his garment with wrong,' says the Lord of hosts" (**Malachi 2:15, 16** NAS). Notice it does not say, "I hate divorce when...." It says plainly that God hates divorce. You can try to justify it in your mind all you want, and the truth will still be that God hates it. A pastor and long-time friend of mine says that he believes that the reason God hates divorce is because marriage on earth is supposed to be a picture of the love Jesus has for His Church and when we get divorces we do damage to the image and portrayal of God and His unending love for His bride. God never ceases to love His bride, even when she became adulterous. If you haven't read Hosea lately you will find that in that short book God calls His people an adulterous bride and still He pursues her and restores her to Himself. So then, the theory of my friend is that when we marry we are conveying a message to the world about God and His love for His bride and when we divorce we are in essence portraying a lie to the world. Remember that marriage is of God and is intended to reveal Him to the world. Still, do not lose heart! Can a person who is divorced be reconciled to God and be forgiven? Of course! If you are divorced, you need to seek God's forgiveness in your life as you would for any other sin, knowing that God's design for your life was not divorce. God IS displeased with divorce, but He WILL forgive you. Set your hope on God and you will not be disappointed. Just be sure you understand what the scripture teaches about divorce. Too often we try to justify our sin. Don't justify it, instead, move on from it and be restored. That may mean that you need to go back to the one you were divorced from and seek reconciliation. It may mean that you need to go and ask forgiveness of the one you divorced or it could mean that you need to forgive the one who divorced you. There is a trend that is growing in America that looks at the first marriage as "practice for the real thing". Many people are getting married without a thought to what it really means and represents and are even approaching it as a temporary study in social behavior. With that, God is not pleased. The texts that cover divorce are few as it only occurs 28 times in the New American Standard Bible, but I encourage you to look them up and study them in their full context.

CHAPTER TWELVE

ONE LOVER PLUS ONE RESPONDER EQUALS PERFECT

As a whole, this will be the section we spend the most time on. It is important that you pay close attention to this section whether you have been married forever or will not be married for forever, whether you are dating, or single. How do we love rightly? Did you know it is laid out very clearly in the Bible? The first thing I will stress is that in a male/female relationship, the man is to be the lover and the woman the responder. This is true in all male/female relationships, though we are primarily looking to the marriage relationship (which I believe is birthed somewhere in the dating relationship. Isn't it true that at some point in dating, hopefully, you come to the realization that you would like to spend the rest of your life with this person?). So what exactly do I mean by this? Well, first of all I am not saying that the woman does not have to love her husband. Remember we have all been called to love each other according to the parameters given us in 1 Corinthians 13. However, in the romantic relationship the man has been created to be the lover and the woman has been created to be the responder. "Husbands, love your wives, just as Christ loved the church and gave himself up for her..." (**Ephesians 5:25**). If you are a Christian, you're part of the church that Christ gave himself up for. In fact, you are called the bride of Christ. Now in the marriage relationship between you and your husband Christ, who loved whom first? The answer is obvious: "we love because he first loved us" (**1 John 4:19**). I know it is because of the love Christ has demonstrated to me that I am involved in the church body, and that I have my own Bible study time. In fact, it is because of the love Jesus holds for me that I desire to do things that are pleasing to Him. What does the Bible tell us in Ephesians? "Husbands, love your wives, just as Christ loved the church..." Gentlemen, we are to be the lovers in the relationship; it's how we were made. I would be willing to bet one of the reasons there are so many divorces today is because men have failed to be lovers. It seems that what always happens when a man fails to be the lover in a relationship is that the woman tries to pick up that role. But the problem is women were not made to be the lovers and men have almost no idea of how to respond. I'll give you an example. I love my friends very much and have occasion to tell them so. Whenever I tell one of my brothers in Christ that I love him, he is quick to reply "I love you too, man." It is not that he does not appreciate or understand the fact that I love him it is just that we as men are not the best responders. My friend Scott and I once spent three hours praying through a large part of the Psalms together. It was an incredible experience. After that time I turned to him and said "That was awesome. You are a good friend. I love you, brother." Now wouldn't it have been weird if he had turned to me and said, "You know, Ryan, I can tell you love me because of the time you spend with me and how nice you are to me and from all the other little things you do."? I probably would have laughed him right out of the apartment. But, in typical male fashion with little emotion attached to it, he simply said. "Yep, good stuff." I didn't take it as an insult it's just how we guys are wired up. If you are still unconvinced, let us take a walk through Song of Songs.

THE BEST SONG EVER SUNG

The book Song of Songs is an excellent example of what I am telling you about the men and women's roles of lover/responder, respectively. First of all, let me point out the title. Both the Hebrew word for "song" and the one for "songs" used here are masculine. The Hebrew word states the song is sung by a masculine voice. Second, the first verse of this book is "Solomon's Song of Songs." Now the woman in the story is the Shulamite. My studies have led me to believe she is either Arabic, or a slave to the Arabic's. Still, we do not find the first verse of this book reading, "The Shulamite's Song of Songs." My point is this:

it is his serenade of her. More than that, it is a song to top all songs; it is a serenade that has never been sung before. He is the one doing the singing. Praise God that He sang a love song to me through Jesus Christ! When I finally heard and understood that song, I was moved to respond to it by coming to Him in salvation. So it was for the Shulamite! She heard this song that was sung for her and it drew her to Solomon. So shall any woman respond to you when you love her correctly. Now, I am not suggesting you will have every woman drawn to your side ready to be your wife. I am certain if God has called you to the married life, it will be to one woman. But this I know for sure, as you love women rightly, they respond. It is as though they have no choice. Don't you find the better you understand the love God holds for you, the more you must respond to it? Men, it is our job to do the singing. It was an old sea legend that sailors would hear a magical song and helplessly point their ships in the direction of it. The legend says it was the song of the siren, one of the most beautiful, and most deadly, women ever. She would sing her song to lure the helpless sailors and their ships to the jagged rocks. Before the sailor knew what was happening, the boat had been smashed to pieces and the ship and its men were done for. As men learn to sing the song, to be the lover, women will respond. The difference will be that you will experience fullness in your relationships and not drowning (perhaps if the old sailors had done the singing like they were supposed to, things would have been different). If you still do not believe me, hang on, we have only discussed the title and the first verse of this rich book.

What I want to show you now is that everything she says is in response to something he has already done. In a similar way, I would like to show you that everything he says comes from pure love. My original walk through these verses was done in the New International Version.

"Let him kiss me with the kisses of his mouth— for your love is more delightful than wine. Pleasing is the fragrance of your perfumes; your name is like perfume poured out" (**Song of Songs 1:2,3**). This is the Shulamite speaking. In the first sentence, she is addressing her friends, or perhaps she is talking to herself. After the sentence break, she is speaking to him, probably directly. She enjoys his kisses and she enjoys the way he smells. Most importantly though, is that his name is like perfume poured out.

If I were to mention the name of someone you do not particularly care for, perhaps you flinch. Maybe you just think to yourself how much you do not like them. Maybe you actually make a repulsive face. By the same token, if I were to mention the name of the person you just cannot get enough of, you would smile. Perhaps even after the name had come and passed in conversation, you would still be lost in a warm fuzzy sort of bliss. The Shulamite enjoys hearing even the name of Solomon; it is like rich perfume poured out. If I put some cologne on before I go out, I smell nice. Yet if I pour out an entire bottle within my home, the entire house will be swept through with pleasing fragrance. When she says his name is like perfume poured out, I imagine he has swept her through and through and that she is completely taken by him. He pleasantly, fully, and completely, overwhelmed her. Now obviously his name isn't like perfume poured out if he is taking advantage of her or being less than gracious to her.

"Take me away with you—let us hurry! Let the king bring me into his chambers"

(**Song of Songs 1:4**). Don't you see it? Can't you hear it in her voice? She wants to be near him! Not because he treats her poorly, but because he honors her. She feels better about herself because of him and what he has said and done. Her confidence has been boosted.

"Dark am I, yet lovely, O daughters of Jerusalem, dark like the tents of Kedar, like the tent curtains of Solomon. Do not stare at me because I am dark, because I am darkened by the sun. My mother's sons were angry with me and made me take care of the vineyards; my own vineyard I have neglected" (**1: 5,6**). Listen to what she is saying as she talks to her friends. "I am dark." Being dark skinned was not always popular like it is now. In fact, fair skin used to be the most attractive feature of a woman. Take a look at all of the Renaissance paintings; all of the women are naked and fair skinned, not a mark on their body. The Shulamite knows that she is less than lovely and it breaks her heart to look at her skin. "I am dark just like all of the tents of Kedar." Kedar is closely associated with Arabia. Every time that Kedar is mentioned in the Bible it seems to be tied to Arabia, much like the Babylonians and Chaldeans seem to be interchangeable in the prophetic books. "I am the same ugly brown as the tents of my people. But then one day King Solomon took me to his tent and I paused, wide-eyed. I am also the same color as the tent curtains of Solomon! Yes, I am dark, but I am lovely." Don't you see the change in her heart? She used to think of herself as plain and ordinary, but after having spent time with Solomon, she has acquired a new view of herself. She is "dark like the tent curtains of Solomon"! He loved her and she has responded! She didn't just change the view she had held of herself all on her own. Something had acted upon her and likely it was the love of Solomon.

"I liken you, my darling, to a mare harnessed to one of the chariots of Pharaoh" (**1:9**). This is the first time Solomon speaks. At first glance it is not very complementary—he is comparing her to a horse—but do not stop at the first glance. There are two ways you can look at what he is saying here; both of which are truly rich compliments. First, we can consider that he is recognizing her as a mare harnessed to the chariot of Pharaoh. Egypt was one of the richest nations at that time, right up until the reign and riches of Solomon; they had somewhere in the neighborhood of 1500 chariots within their army and many more for trading and export purposed. Most chariots were drawn by a team of horses. Every reference I have found refers to a team, and since I do not know how many horses are on a chariot team, we will limit the number to two. Let us suppose that Pharaoh has 3000 horses plus for his chariots; Solomon is comparing the Shulamite to one of them. If Pharaoh only used stallions to pull his chariots, Solomon is saying his love stands out like one mare among 2999 stallions. If in fact Pharaoh used both stallions and mares, Solomon is still recognizing her as one of the best of his 3000 horses. (A friend of mine, after having heard me teach this, went and looked into Egyptian practices and found that Pharaoh would always use stallions, and that mares were never even allowed into battle. Clearly, she is occupying a place none before her have held.) Solomon wanted and had the best of everything; every three years, ships would come from all over the world with apes, gold, silver, jewels, ivory, food and spices (**1 Kings 10:22**). Only the best was good enough for this king. We also know that he imported his chariots and horses, some from Egypt (**1 Kings 10:28,29**). The second view we can take on this is one where Solomon sees something that he must have and goes after it. Knowing that Solomon will only take the best, and the fact that he pursues—and ends up married to—the Shulamite, we can see how this statement is very complementary. Whatever he means by it, I feel certain he is voicing recognition of her beauty and her talent.

"How handsome you are, my lover. Oh, how charming! And our bed is verdant" (**1: 16**). This perhaps is a verse you have missed or skipped over because you did not want to look up the word "verdant." Never again will you have to miss it, because I have looked up this word for you. It means: green, growing, and leafy. When I read these first definitions, I about fell out of my seat; luckily, it does not stop there. It also means, "Unripe in experience or judgment." How wonderful it was that their bed was unripe in experience! You see that their marriage relationship was new and fresh! Men, as the lovers in the relationship, it is imperative that we always seek to keep the marriage bed holy. **(Hebrews 13:4)**

"The beams of our house are cedars; our rafters are firs" **(1:17)**. This is Solomon again, and here he seems to be saying their house is strong. What is interesting is they are not yet married. Still Solomon has apparently had the house made ready. Perhaps as the lover, men should, figuratively speaking, build a strong house in which their wife can live. I prayed and prepared for 10 years before I ever even met my wife so that I could ensure that she would have a safe and strong and stable home. What kind of home are you preparing for your family?

If you still doubt these roles, please note that twenty-six times the Shulamite refers to Solomon as her "lover." Solomon, on the other hand, calls her darling, dove, precious one, sister, and bride. Never does he call her his "lover," because she is not.

Guys, it is important that you tell her how much you love her, and also that you show it. Words are nothing but arrogance if they are not followed with action. I say this because if you think you can tell a woman you love her but never show her, and you expect her to respond just because of who you are, then you are full of pride and you will be sorely disappointed.

"I am a rose of Sharon, a lily of the valleys."

"Like a lily among thorns is my darling among the maidens" **(2:1,2)**. The Shulamite refers to herself as a flower among flowers, but her lover is quick to correct her and point out that she is like a flower among thorns. We see again that Solomon is always ready to tell of how she stands out richly to him.

In the next nine verses, the Shulamite goes on and on about her lover. She says he is like an "apple tree among the trees of the forest," and that she "delights in his shade" and his fruit is "sweet to her taste" (**2:3**). Here she is saying he stands out among men, that he protects her (represented by the shade) and that he provides for her (the fruit that is sweet to her taste). He has taken her "to the banquet hall, and his banner is love" (**2:4**). She asks that she be "strengthened with apples and raisins" for she "is faint with love" (**2:5**). It is somewhat nice to know that women, like men, can be made weak in the knees by love. "His left arm is under my head and his right arm embraces me" (**2:6**). In verse seven of chapter two, she charges her friends to "not arouse or awaken love until it so desires." I think this is a particularly important warning to our high school, college, and single age groups. So many people are on the warpath seeking out their one true love that they often forget to wait for God. The Shulamite will warn her friends this way several more times. Then she sees her lover and she becomes ecstatic (**2:8,9**). He speaks to her saying she should go with him and that the "winter is past; the rains are over and gone. Flowers appear on the earth; the season of singing has come, the cooing of doves is heard in our land. The fig tree forms its early fruit; the blossoming vines spread their fragrance. Arise, come, my darling; my beautiful one, come with me"

(**2:10-13**). What beautiful verses; it talks of spring and new life! What a great picture we have here of what God has in store for us.

"Show me your face, let me hear your voice; for your voice is sweet, and your face lovely" (**2:14**). I find it great that he wants to hear her voice. You know what it's like when the phone rings and you answer it and on the other end is the most wonderful voice you have ever heard. Or when you happen to be in a crowded room, and somewhere above the noise you catch a word or two, perhaps a laugh of the one your heart loves, and as you examine each face, your eyes finally rest upon her beautiful visage. This is how Solomon feels. If you are married and you feel like it's been a while since you have had the longing for your spouse's voice or face then perhaps you have not been making time to be together. Turn off the TV, and go on a date. Get into bed before you are tired, and just spend a few minutes talking about the days that you have had. But if this longing is missing in your relationship, then do what it takes to restore it.

"Catch for us the foxes, the little foxes that ruin the vineyards, our vineyards that are in bloom" (**2:15**). This is Solomon's plea to guard against all the little things that fight against a Godly and joyful relationship. Very seldom is it the large and ugly things that build walls in relationships; the Great Wall of China did not spring up over night. Rather, brick was laid upon brick. In the same way it is a lot of "little foxes" that will bring ruin to the "vineyard." In other words, it is all the little things that steal the joy. The large things come with a lot of pomp and circumstance.

We know when there is a large issue to deal with. We know when the world is falling apart. But those aren't the most deadly things. The most deadly things are the seemingly insignificant things that will, in the end, cause our death or the death of our marriages.

"My lover is mine and I am his; he browses among the lilies. Until the day breaks and the shadows flee, turn, my lover, and be like a gazelle or like a young stag on the hills of Bether" (**2:16,17**). It is the night before the wedding, and, quite frankly, the Shulamite is talking to her friends. It is important to know that the hills of Bether were twin mountains. Basically what the bride is telling her friends is she longs for her bridegroom to be like a gazelle on her twin mountains. In plain English, she desires that he would play with and fondle her breasts. We perhaps cringe at that word fondle, but God made the body to be a delight within a marriage relationship and even tells the husband to be pleased to be satisfied in the breasts of his wife (**Proverbs 5:19**).

Chapter three continues the tale of the night before the wedding; we find that the bride-to-be is unable to sleep and even gets up and wanders around the city to see if she can find the one her heart loves. When she does, she is unwilling to let him go. We also find in this chapter, beginning in verse 6, a picture of the wedding procession. Perhaps Solomon is coming to receive his bride. Somewhere between chapters three and four the wedding takes place.

Chapter four tells of the wedding night! He describes her eyes, hair, teeth, lips, mouth, temples, neck and breasts. He delights in his wife. When describing how lovely she is he compares her to flocks and sheep and goats. This is because one of the primary trades of Kedar was shepherding and he knows she can understand and identify with it. "Your neck is like the tower of David, built with elegance; on it hang a thousand shields, all of them shields of warriors" (**4:4**). This verse baffled me for a long time until I came across a couple of verses in Ezekiel. I will go into more detail later when we talk about the role of the husband, but for now, let me say that he is telling of how far and wide her fame spreads and how all people revere her. He tells her how beautiful she is and how "there is no flaw in [her]" (**4:7**). He calls her his sister and bride and tells of how she has stolen his heart with one glance of her eyes (**4:9**). (I pause only long enough to say that women do possess some sort of unbelievable talent with their eyes. They seem to look at you in a certain way, and, truthfully, you become weak. Any man who says differently is either lying or has never met a woman that he looked in the eyes.) He tells her how she is a garden locked up. It would seem they have waited until the wedding night to have sex. In verses 12-15 of this chapter he describes, in my opinion, what he expects to find in her "garden". "You are a spring enclosed, a sealed fountain. Your plants are an orchard... with choice fruits..., with every kind of incense tree, and all the finest spices."(**4:13,14**) He is excited, but is more concerned with loving her. I know this because he does not make a move to have sex with her until she has invited him to do so. When he is describing her garden as being locked up he is talking about her most intimate parts. He recognizes that he does not have the key to open this "garden" but that the owner must open it. I think it is fantastic that he does not pressure her into sex on the wedding night just because it is expected. But being a man of integrity he waits. Then the Shulamite responds favorably "Awake, north wind, and come, south wind! Blow on my garden, that its fragrance may spread abroad. Let my lover come into his garden and taste its choice fruits."(**4:16**) Here she invites him into her. She opens the garden to him that he may experience the fullness of the marriage bed. Later he answers her "I have come into my garden, my sister, my bride..."(**5:1**) and we see that the couple has delighted in the physical aspect of sex in the marriage bed.

If you think that was awesome, check out how he treats her at the end of chapter five and the beginning of chapter six. What has happened is he has gone to her bedchamber, probably for sex with his wife. However, she is already in bed and has washed her feet and does not want to get up. Since she does not answer her door he leaves, but as he does he drops some myrrh on the door handle. Just a moment passes before the young bride's heart pounds for her lover and she throws open the door to find the perfume on the handle but her lover gone. After a brief search, during which she has woken some of her friends, and an arrest by the officials of the palace, she finds Solomon in the garden of the palace. It is dark and the night air is cool and wet. As she approaches he hears and turns, and she stops silent to hear his complaint or rebuke. "You are beautiful, my darling..." Wow!

He sees his wife and is not and never was upset. He was happy to let her sleep, but is happier to see her now. I think perhaps the moon must have been out and been full, because Solomon can see her eyes (not to mention that he probably had his arms tightly around her) and they overwhelm him so much he forgets what he wanted to say. "You are beautiful, my darling, as Tirzah, lovely as Jerusalem, majestic as troops with banners. Turn your eyes from me; they overwhelm me."(6:4,5) Then he continues on about her hair, teeth, temples, and calls her his "perfect one". Do you notice anything here? He does not get sexual with her. He went to her bed-chamber for sex, gets put off, she comes to find him, and all he says is how beautiful she is and how much he loves her. On the honeymoon he looks over her whole body and delights in it but here he doesn't go below the shoulders as he describes her beauty. Its as if he wants her to know that he loves her no matter what and that his pursuit of her is not a sexual one. He does not even mention the incident. Wow! He continues to tell her that there may be sixty queens and eighty concubines and virgins without number but she is his perfect one and is unique. (6:8,9)

Chapter seven is, I think, a chapter dedicated to the joy in delighting in the body and the sexual relationship between a man and a woman. I believe that Solomon is staring at the naked body of his beloved and it is because of how close he is to her both emotionally and physically that he is overcome with words for her. Solomon begins at her feet and then speaks of her legs. He talks about how her navel is full of wine and her waist a mound of wheat encircled by lilies, thus expressing his joy with that part of her body. He continues his journey up to her breasts and her neck. Then, he takes a moment to be captivated by her face and speaks of her eyes, nose, and her head including her hair. "Your hair is like royal tapestry; the king is held captive by its tresses." (**7:5**) The idea here is that her hair is so enticing to him that it almost literally has him tied up. He tells her how pleasing she is and describes her stature as a palm tree and her breasts as fruit and he tells himself that he desires to climb the tree and take hold of her fruit. "May your breasts be like the clusters of the vine, the fragrance of your breath like apples, and your mouth like the best wine."(**7:8,9**) Finally he has finished his soliloquy. Then she responds and tells of how she desires to be with him and she even invites him on what we might call a romantic weekend getaway. (**7:11-13**).

I want to draw your attention to two more things before we leave this book: One, I want to take you to Chapter 8 verses six and seven. "Place me like a seal over your heart, like a seal on your arm; for love is as strong as death, its jealousy unyielding as the grave. It burns like a blazing fire, like a mighty flame. Many waters cannot quench love; rivers cannot wash it away. If one were to give all the wealth of his house for love, it would be utterly scorned." Love is permanent like death and is to be a fire that no waters can put out. In fact perhaps a more accurate translation of this verse concerning the part about the fire would be this; Love is "a vehement flame of the Lord."

You see, when a man and woman are joined together under God it is not a human fire, but God's vehement flame that burns their hearts and melts them to one. It is so valuable that no price can buy it.

But there is one more example I would like to show you. Remember at the bachelorette party, the Shulamite says "turn, my lover, and be like a gazelle or like a young stag on the rugged hills" (Or the hills of Bether, which, again, were twin mountains) (**2:17**). She is talking to herself, or to her friends, and saying how much she longs for him to caress her. On the wedding night he tells her he will go to the mountain and to the hill until day breaks. In other words, she gets her wish. But stop for a moment and consider the last two verses of this book. I will set up what I believe is happening. There is a party of sorts in the garden of the palace. He is talking to his friends and she to hers. Finally, he looks up and sees her across the way. Her hair is beautiful, and the way she moves is so graceful. She laughs and he smiles as he watches her. The voices of his friends fall on deaf ears, until he excuses himself and walks up to his wife—who is in the middle of a rich conversation with her friends. He leans over and whispers in her ear as he places his hand on the back of her head. "You who dwell in the gardens. The companions listen for your voice—Let me hear it" (**8:13**). She smiles because she knows he is sincere; she leans next to his face and her cheek is on his. Quietly she whispers back, "Make haste, my lover, and be like a gazelle or a young stag on the mountains of spice" (**8:14**). Wow! Basically what happened was he wanted to hear the lovely voice of his wife, but because he was so sincere and loved her so well, she tells him to be a gazelle on the mountains of spice. Again in plain English, she invites him not only to talk to her, but also to caress her and be delighted in her body and specifically her breasts. He just wanted to hear her voice and now he gets even more than that. I believe this couple excused themselves from the party. She told her friends Solomon was not feeling well. He told his friends his wife was growing tired. The two of them went upstairs and to bed; but not to sleep. How awesome it is that he has loved her and she has responded.

I know this walk through Song of Songs has not been complete or in depth, but I hope now you can see a little more clearly there is a role of the lover and the responder. That is what I set out to show you in this section, and it is time to move on. However, you will find that many of our remaining sections will bring us back to Song of Solomon. There is still so much to cover. So much about love that we have yet to learn! But how exciting that the Bible is our textbook and the Spirit our teacher!!

CHAPTER THIRTEEN

THE UNIQUE TREASURE

4-14-03

My dear wonderful wife, wherever you are, whoever you are;

I have always known you would be unique. I am guilty of having thought girls were unique in the past, girls that were not you. I have sought to love them, and in hindsight I see that they are of the mold of all other girls. It was never them I really wanted, it was you. "Sixty queens" there may be, but you surpass them all. "Eighty concubines" may run around the earth and pass me by day by day, but you are above all unique. Hardly a day passes when you do not fill my mind. Let me tell you how you are unique to me now, here in your absence, here in my ignorance of you. I travel almost 3000 miles a month preaching. There is not a trip taken where I fail to look into the empty passenger seat of my car. It is a place I have reserved for you. No one else could ever fill it. I imagine you (as best I can without face or form) sleeping in that seat as we drive home from a particularly exhausting weekend in ministry. The sun lights up your face. I want to reach over and touch you, but I don't want to wake you. Sweetheart, I don't know where you are, but I know you uniquely will fill that role. Every time I preach, I look to the front row of the church. You should be there. Anyone else could be there and I wouldn't care. You being there will fill me with more hope and confidence than I have ever known; your smile will cause me to preach the word of God with excitement. When I am writing a sermon, I imagine you standing over my shoulder deleting and adding points as you see fit. I've thought of waking up to you in the morning. I've thought of laughing with you as we enjoy life. I've thought of holding you and smelling your perfume on my clothes for hours afterward. Right now on the top shelf of my closet I have cards that I have bought you over the years that are addressed to "My Beloved" and I have a stack of t-shirts I call my "wife t-shirts." They are the ones too small for me or the ones I wore for eight years before they became so faded and worn they could hardly stand the strain of daily wear. I imagine you wearing them to bed or to lounge on the couch while you read your book or magazine. It is only you who could fill this longing in my heart. God has been preparing me for you and you for me. Who but you could make me happy? Who but you could pray for me before I go to preach the way you will? Who could love me and encourage me like you will when I grow weary in ministry? You are unique! There is none for me but you! I love you and long to know you. I pray that God will bring you swiftly to me. You are my unique one and I long to remind you of that every day! Until then,

ryan

ONE WHO IS UNIQUE

This section is inspired by a verse in Song of Solomon, but I felt it deserved its own heading. Perhaps owing to the very personal meaning it has to me right now. Here I am two years into writing this, and over three years into study and I find myself continually learning more about it all, and yet still ignorant of so much. "But my dove, my perfect one, is unique, the only daughter of her mother, the favorite of the one who bore her. The maidens saw her and called her blessed; the queens and concubines praised her" (**Song of Songs 6:9**). I guess I will begin rambling and try to put into words what this means to me and what it should mean to you. First of all, this is Solomon speaking. Hopefully you were able to gather that from the text, but it is important to know. Solomon finds his "dove," his "perfect one," "unique." Wow! What a complement. I will start by addressing the men, and second the women, with the understanding that everything I have said to this point and everything I will say from this point on is pertinent to both men and women. Men, you should feel that your dove is unique. She should stand out to you. But more importantly, you are responsible to let her know she is unique. I have learned this of late. Tell her what it is about her that makes her special to you, a one-of-a-kind woman. Is it the fact that her love for God inspires you? Perhaps her love for people? Maybe it's that she seems to understand you where no one else has ever been able to. Could it be her eyes captivate you? Do you stutter when you speak to her because she leaves you breathless? Whatever it is, you need to let her know. Ladies, don't settle for a man to whom you are not unique. Do not sell yourself short of that which is right. If you are one of many to him, one who offers to him what everyone else does, how does that bless you? Be blessed of God by being with a man who finds you special and unique and who lets you know about it. The more I consider "unique," the more I am caught up in what it means. Consider this definition of unique: "Being the only one of its kind, sole, single. Being without or having no equal or like, singular." The sin in so many of us, the shortcoming, is that we have said "this person is unique to me," then we break up and move on. Later in life we find another and say, "No, this is the one who is unique." With time though, this special one—this "unique" individual—is gone from our lives and we turn to someone else. By the time we end up in a serious relationship and married, we have called half a dozen people unique. Perhaps this does not bother you, but it does me. If someone is truly unique to us, they cannot be replaced no matter how long you look or how extensive your search may be. When the Bible indicates are to find one who is unique to us, it does not mean to find a dozen unique individuals. (Which, according to the very definition of unique isn't even possible.) It means we would find one who is unique. Truly some of you are raising the argument that all people are unique in some form and that all relationships are unique. While in words this is true, it is not true when we look at it in regards to our spouse. Be careful not to call one your husband who may not be your husband. Be careful not to call one your wife who may not be your wife. Slow down a bit and with patient prayerful pursuit seek out the **One Who Is Unique.**

THE TREASURE HUNTER
3-20-03
My Beautiful Crown,

It is hard for me to seek you; I have often given up the hope of ever finding you. Sometimes I wish it were easier. To be honest, I haven't even considered you much over the last few months for fear I would come to the realization that you were not to be found. But my heart longs for you so much. And now in the snowy mountains of Colorado my heart longs for you. I have new resolve to take up the search again. I must find you! I can't stand to be without you much longer. You truly are my crown; you are what will make me shine. I hardly know how it is that I could have ever considered not continuing the search for you. But with all discipline, I will search you out. I will find you and you will adorn me and together we will seek and serve our God.

ryan

It is by a strong sense of duty and obligation that I add this section to the mix. I confess there is a part of me that does not really like the truth of this section, but I say this only in jest or in cowardice—I am not sure which one is most prevalent. In light of what we have just learned from Solomon, we know that men are to be the lovers and women the responders. So what is this whole treasure hunter thing about? In Proverbs we are told that an "excellent wife is the crown of her husband" (**12:4**). However, we are later told that "he who finds a wife finds a good thing, and obtains favor from the Lord" (**Proverbs 18:22**). Now, I do not believe it to be a commonly known truth, but the fact is that most (if not all) guys are cowards when it comes to asking out a girl. It is true now and will be every day from now on. We are terrified. One of my first encounters with girls was in first grade; I had a crush on this lovely little blonde and as it turned out she liked my friend. That was all it took. A touch of rejection and I am forever terrified of the prospect of asking a girl out. By the time I was in second grade and had a crush on a girl I was doomed to insecurity. I wrote a note to her one day that said, "I like you". She wrote back, "I like you too." To which my great fears and doubts responded, again by note, "no you don't, you're just playing a joke on me". Obviously it didn't take me long to be fearful of the fairer sex. Now the man who has no fear has either never experienced rejection, has never been wowed by a woman, or has some loose circuits upstairs.

A woman must have invented Caller Id because no sensible man would do such a thing. It used to be that a man could dial a girl's number, let the phone ring once or twice, and hang up. Palms sweating and heart thundering so loud he can't hear his buddies yelling out "c'mon, man, you can do it!" I remember the days of calling three or four times before you actually ever said anything. Now you cannot call and hang up because your name and number are already given to her. Sure, there have been times I wished it was the other way around. That the girls would call, that they would initiate. But the Bible teaches that a man finds the wife, and if God leads him, he finds a crown! So men, buck up! Dust yourself off, patch up all the old wounds, and find her! Seek her out!

Ladies, there will be some of you who do not have the patience to be found. You would put a big neon sign over your head blaring "available" if you could. I encourage you to allow yourself to be found by a man. Don't put yourself in a position to be found, just wait and be found. Remember the summer nights as a kid when we would play Hide-n-seek? Remember when you were in your hiding spot waiting for the seeker's eyes to fall upon you and then you would dash to home base? Some of you women just don't like hiding and much prefer the chase, so you jump out and yell "olli olli oxen free" and try to get caught. If we do it the way God has designed, the men would seek, the women would wait, and at the right time the woman will be found and the man will be crowned! How blessed it is to find the crown that God has hidden for me!

CHAPTER FOURTEEN

I DON'T HATE THIS PART OF MARRIED LIFE

ONE TO DELIGHT IN

3-20-03

My Dear Precious Wife,

I don't know how to start a note to you about our most intimate of encounters. I know that often I have thought of that time that I would come with you to our verdant bed. I want you to know I have waited for you for this moment. You and I will share this time together and it will be a sacred place, a sacred time. What we whisper here, I will cherish and hold on to; it is not for others. My delight in your body and yours in mine will be a secret treasure shared between us. I do love you. I pray God would bring you quickly to me. I long to hold your hand and kiss

143

your mouth. I can't wait to hold you tightly to me. Oh, that God would speed you to me.

ryan

I do not think I can emphasize enough the importance of not selling yourself short of what God has planned for you in marriage. Do not settle for the here-and-now when God has told you to wait. I believe you should be enamoured by the very one God brings into your life. You know when you were a kid, or younger than you are now, or yesterday, when that "special someone" accidentally touched your hand, and shivers ran a marathon up and down your spine? Remember how your voice cracked when you tried to approach the subject of romantic interest? I will give you an example. I am one who is quite comfortable speaking to and in front of others. In public speaking in college, I was so at ease that I would write my speech half an hour before class, go in without having practiced once, and wow both the other students and my professor. Even so, the last several times I have tried to let a girl know I was interested in her, my tongue would seem to swell so much in my mouth that I would stutter and stumble over my words. All of the sudden my voice becomes weak and starts cracking. It is a feeling of anticipation, overwhelming fear, and joy wrapped up in one. How about the time you lock eyes with someone either right next to you, or across a crowded room? You know how you both seem to smile and one of you—if not both—look shyly at the ground as the temperature above your shirt collar rises several points on the thermometer? How about the last time you received a fireworks kiss and you went temporarily stupid? A friend of mine once asked if I had ever experienced a fireworks kiss and went on to tell me this that type of kiss was one where your spine tingled and leapt out the front of your chest. At the point that he asked me this question, I had not yet had such an experience, but when I did; it was as though my brain would not work, my eyes would not see, and my ears could not hear. I was overwhelmed and floating on delight. And that kiss was just a peck placed softly on my cheek. The only other fireworks kiss I had was when a kiss was laid on my palm, then my thumb. It may sound weird to you, but I can tell you that though it was over a year ago, I can still feel that kiss on my hand. It warms my heart and is a sweet fragrance to my nostrils. It is my firm opinion that God has designed our marriage life to be like this, not for just a moment, but rather for a lifetime. Let us look and see what Scripture has to say about this feeling, this warmth, this walking on air. We will cover a lot of the passages that we saw just a moment ago in Song of Solomon, but I really feel we need to look at them in greater detail and catch a glimpse of the delight God has in store for us when we submit to His plan for our lives in marriage.

"Rejoice in the wife of your youth. As a loving hind and a graceful doe, let her breasts satisfy you at all times; be exhilarated (intoxicated) always with her love." (**Proverbs 5:18-19**) So here is what we are looking at, the right of the man to delight in his wife.

I am so glad that these verses are in the Bible. What a great command of God. Not only does He give us a wife as a blessing but also then He instructs us to be satisfied with her breasts and to be intoxicated with her love. The man is told to rejoice in his wife. This does not sound as though the marriage relationship is supposed to simply drone on day by day. Let us look at some of the things Solomon says to his wife.

"How beautiful you are, my darling! Oh, how beautiful! Your eyes are doves" (**Song of Songs 1:15**). This is one of many times that Solomon tells his wife how beautiful she is. Also, we see here, as we do throughout Song of Solomon, that he is taken with her eyes. There is definitely something to be said about looking longingly into the eyes of the one you love. It is almost mind numbing.

"How beautiful you are my darling! Oh, how beautiful! Your eyes behind your veil are doves. Your hair is like a flock of goats descending from Mount Gilead. Your teeth are like a flock of sheep just shorn, coming up from the washing. Each has its twin; not one of them is alone. Your lips are like a scarlet ribbon; your mouth is lovely. Your temples behind your veil are like the halves of a pomegranate. Your neck is like the tower of David, built with elegance; on it hang a thousand shields, all of them shields of warriors. Your two breasts are like two fawns, like twin fawns of a gazelle that browse among the lilies. Until the day breaks and the shadows flee, I will go to the mountain of myrrh and to the hill of incense. All beautiful you are, my darling; there is no flaw in you. You have stolen my heart, my sister, my bride; you have stolen my heart with one glance of your eyes, with one jewel of your necklace. How delightful is your love, my sister, my bride! How much more pleasing is your love than wine, and the fragrance of your perfume than any spice! Your lips drop sweetness as the honeycomb, my bride; milk and honey are under your tongue. The fragrance of your garments is like that of Lebanon." (**SOS 4:1-7,9-11**)

It is important to remember when reading the above passage that the reason Solomon compares his wife's features to that of flocks is because she probably grew up around flocks and therefore can identify with what he is saying. Note here how he says her eyes have stolen his heart. We can tell he loves her mouth, and probably kissing her mouth, by his words that her "lips drop sweetness" and "milk and honey are under your tongue."

"How beautiful your sandaled feet... Your graceful legs are like jewels... your navel is a rounded goblet that never lacks blended wine. Your waist is a mound of wheat encircled by lilies. Your breasts are like two fawns, twins of a gazelle. Your neck is like an ivory tower. Your eyes are pools... your nose is like the tower of Lebanon... Your head crowns you like Mount Carmel. Your hair is like royal tapestry; the king is held captive by its tresses. How beautiful you are and how pleasing, o love, with your delights! Your stature is like that of the palm, and your breasts like clusters of fruit. 'I will climb the palm tree; I will take hold of its fruit.' May your breasts be like the clusters of the vine, the fragrance of your breath like apples, and your mouth like the best wine." **(Song of Solomon 7:1-9)**

I think perhaps of all he says to her, this passage is close to—if not the most—intimate. He describes her from the bottom of her feet to the top of her head; he leaves nothing out. I believe when he equates her navel and her waist with things like wine and wheat, he is speaking of her in a very personal and sexual way. He finds great joy and fulfillment in her body. He is satisfied with it and by it. He indicates that in the same way as he would be satisfied with wheat and wine, so he is satisfied with her navel and waist. These are undoubtedly sexual references. We also see that he even tells himself he wants to take hold of her breasts. This is not an ancient custom of eastern cultures; rather, it is an intimate expression of joy and delight intended for sexual pleasure.

Now let's look at what the woman has to say about delighting in her husband. We have already looked at much of what she has to say, but again I believe it bears repeating.

"Let him kiss me with the kisses of his mouth-for your love is more delightful than wine" (**Song of Solomon 1:2**). This one is just plain obvious. She likes to be kissed by him.

"My lover is to me a sachet of myrrh resting between my breasts" (**Song of Solomon 1:13**). I think that we put cologne or perfume on not only because we want people to think we smell nice, but also because we enjoy the fragrance. Either way we can see her husband-to-be is a beautiful fragrance to her.

"Strengthen me with raisins, refresh me with apples, for I am faint with love" (**Song of Solomon 2:5**). As I have already stated, it is good to know that women can become weak with love. That is what has happened here. She has the beating of her heart, the flush of her face, and the weakness of her legs to let her know she is in love with this man.

"Until the day breaks and the shadows flee, turn, my lover, and be like a gazelle or like a young stag on the rugged hills." (**Song of Solomon 2:17**) We find here she desires to have the touch of her husband upon her body, particularly her breasts.

"Scarcely had I passed them when I found the one my heart loves. I held him and would not let him go till I had brought him to my mother's house, to the room of the one who conceived me" (**Song of Solomon 3:4**). Do you see how much she loves him? She loves him so much that she does not want to let him go from her.

"My lover thrust his hand through the latch-opening; my heart began to pound for him" (**Song** of Solomon 5:4**). The sound of her lover's voice and the thought of him cause her heart to pound for him because she delights in him.

"I opened for my lover, but my lover had left; he was gone. My heart sank at his departure" (**Song of Solomon 5:6**). She opens the door with the anticipation of gazing on her lover, only to find he is gone. If she did not delight in him so much, there would be no reason for her heart to sink at his departure.

> "My lover is radiant and ruddy, outstanding among ten thousand. His head is purest gold; his hair is wavy and black as a raven. His eyes are like doves by the water streams, washed in milk, mounted like jewels. His cheeks are like beds of spice yielding perfume. His lips are like lilies dripping with myrrh. His arms are rods of gold set with chrysolite. His body is like polished ivory decorated with sapphires. His legs are pillars of marble set on bases of pure gold. His appearance is like Lebanon, choice as its cedars. His mouth is sweetness itself; he is altogether lovely. This is my lover, this my friend, oh daughters of Jerusalem." (**Song of Solomon 5:10-16**)

Though I would say it seems as though women are not as concerned with the physical appearance as men are, it is evident by this passage that it is appropriate for the woman to delight in the body of her husband. She praises him as one that stands out among ten thousand. His head, or his face, is like gold to her. His features captivate her; in this case, his black curly hair and his beautiful eyes. Have you noticed how she even likes his cheeks? We find that his lips drip with her favorite perfume. She admires his arms and his body is to her like ivory decorated with sapphires (possibly his nipples). She considers his legs as marble and his feet as gold. She compares him to the cedars of Lebanon, the choicest wood of all, used for building palaces and temples. Again she tells of how his mouth is sweetness to her and that he is completely lovely to her. Probably the greatest delight she has in him though, is that he is not only her lover but also her friend.

The point I desire to make in all of this is we are designed to delight in the person and physical body of the one God joins us to in marriage. We should look, be awed, and give praise and glory to God for the gift He has bestowed upon us. We are not only allowed, but also encouraged, to take joy in the body of our spouse, to delight in knowing it and seeing it and experiencing it. Hear the words of God to the newly married couple (though some translators believe these to be the friends of the bride and groom speaking to the newly married couple): "Eat, O friends, and drink; drink your fill, O lovers."

Thank you, God, for the gift of delight!

DELIGHT! BUT NOT YET!

I think it is imperative that I come quickly with this section; especially as it is on the heels of the one above. This section is intended for those who are not married. Even if your wedding day is tomorrow, you are as of yet unmarried and this is to you.

While it is clearly true that God has designed a man to delight in the body of his wife and a woman to delight in the body of her husband, we must be sure that we don't seek out that body too early. Let me try to help you understand what I mean. There is a delight of man and there is a delight of God. Obviously, when we experience the delight of God it is richer, deeper, and of greater value to us than when we experience our own delights. So often what happens in a dating and/or engaged relationship is that we begin to kiss too much. That leads us to pressing bodies against each other. I don't want to be graphic, but I do want to convey the crippling truth of pursuing what we call delight rather than what God has in store for us. Eventually, pressing and rubbing bodies together is not enough to satisfy the sinful cravings of our flesh. Hands venture up shirts or down pants and before we know how we got there exactly, perhaps we are naked with that one we say we hold so dear. You could argue (especially if you are engaged) that you are just delighting in the body that is going to be yours anyway. You could tell me how great if feels to kiss and touch and all those other things, but what you are doing is robbing yourself of the delight God has in store for you. First of all, as a Christian couple you know that you are not honoring God when your physical relationship becomes one that is fulfilling your own cravings for physical elation. But think about it. If a man views breasts in a sinful way his whole life, he gets hung up on pornography where women have breasts bared. Inevitably he feels guilty. Then as he gets into a relationship, he fondles and views his girlfriend's breasts, and then it only continues when he gets engaged. And inevitably he feels guilty some more. How many of those times was he delighting in the body of a woman the way God designed? The answer is, of course, none. Since we are a people of conditional responses and learned behavior, here is the end result of physical things as sin in our lives. A man such as I have just described above gets married one day. Now on his wedding night, he is given the opportunity to take complete delight in the breasts of his wife. But if he has always dealt with breasts in a sinful way, he will not be able to fully enjoy his wife on the wedding night. He has trained himself over the years. Every time he saw breasts prior to marriage it triggered a guilt response. Now here he is married and supposed to be enjoying the breasts of his wife, but sinful patterns prevail and his initial response is guilt. Don't think that you can participate in sinful physical behavior now and that it will have no affect on your marriage relationship. Let me explain it this way. So many people today get married and breathe a sigh of relief. They struggled so hard with the physical relationship it was everything they could do to get married without having sex. They get married as virgins, but they also get married having done virtually everything up to the point of having sex, so when they get married, they cry out with a sigh of relief, "oh, we made it!" But they really haven't made it. Their entire physical relationship has been sin, and now they expect that they can fully enjoy each other's bodies the way God intended. It cannot happen. If every day a persistent child put his hand on the hot stove only to find it burned, then there may come a time the child would be cautious about touching a stove that was clearly not hot. In a similar manner, when we fall under conviction and guilt every time we enter into sinful physical behavior and we enter into that behavior up to marriage, we cannot expect to have full joy in the marriage bed. Contrasting the couple who gets married with a sigh of relief is a couple I know; when I had this talk with them, they realized God wanted them to be physically pure until marriage. At least the last nine months of their engaged life they honored God in their bodies. About two weeks after their honeymoon, I received a call from the husband; he told me how fantastic their honeymoon had been. He thanked me for sharing with him this biblical concept of delight. His wife got on the phone and expressed how grateful she was and how it had made such a difference in their marriage bed to enter into it with pure hearts. Just today I called to make sure I could refer to them in my writing, and the wife emphatically approved. She said, "Please tell people. It has made such a difference. Use our names if you want, we don't care." Out of courtesy to my friends I will not use their names, but I will tell you that because they made their relationship one that honored God in body, they are now abundantly blessed in their marriage. Others I have shared this with have said they would work at being pure physically, and I continue to see them struggle. Yet this one couple made a solemn vow to God to honor Him. It was that important to them and they did not break that vow; now they are reaping their reward in marriage.

I wish I could say it a hundred times over. Be pure physically until marriage. If you have not been pure up to this point, then begin again today. Do not approach it casually. Do not think in your heart that you will "try" to be pure. Know that God has commanded you to be pure and that He has enabled you to do so. This is not so you will have no fun, but for your blessing in a marriage relationship that the fun of the marriage bed would overflow with delight for you and your spouse.

CHAPTER FIFTEEN

WANTED: PEOPLE WHO DO THEIR JOB

In the world today, roles have become obsolete. Everyone is inclined to do what they feel will work for them. Specific guidelines have been cast out and when someone does live by those guidelines, they are "odd" or "close-minded." But God laid out roles for us to follow and He made us to be inclined toward them. What you think will work for you alone will eventually fail and you will be forced to find something else. The guidelines that have been cast out and called outdated by our culture are the very ones that will be life to you, and will, as you observe them, birth life in you. I feel it is very important as I show you what the Bible says about the role of the husband and wife that you pay close attention. Guys, look as hard at what God says about the woman as you would your own role. This will give you a better understanding of who she is. Ladies, find out what

God says about what the man you are to marry looks like. This will help you to understand what he must be about.

A SUITABLE HELPER

I begin with the woman, the wife, the "suitable helper." "The Lord God said, 'it is not good for the man to be alone. I will make a helper suitable for him.'... But for Adam no suitable helper was found" (**Genesis 2:18, 20**).

Now, there are a few things you should know. First of all, there are seven forms of a Hebrew verb; the simple form is the Kal. The particular form for the word "help" in this verse is the Hiphil. The Hiphil is the cause of the Kal. For example, if a sentence in your Old Testament says "to go forth" and it happens to be the Hiphil form, what it is really saying is "to bring or lead forth." Other examples are "to be holy," (Kal) "to sanctify/ to make holy," (Hiphil) "to perish," (Kal) "to destroy." (Hiphil) Again, the Hiphil is the cause of the help, or the means by which the verb takes place. Second, this particular word in this form is used only 21 times in the Old Testament. Because I think it is important, I am going to give you the other verses in their entirety (that way you have no excuse for having not read them). You have already seen the two in Genesis.

Speaking of Moses' son: "and the other was named Eliezer, for he said, 'My father's God was my **helper**; He saved me from the sword of Pharaoh' " (**Exodus 18:4**).

" 'Hear, O Lord, the cry of Judah; bring him to his people. With his own hands he defends his cause. Oh, be his **help** against his foes' " (**Deuteronomy 33:7**).

" 'There is no one like the God of Jeshurun, who rides on the heavens to **help** you and on the clouds in his majesty' " (**Deuteronomy 33:26**).

" 'Blessed are you, O Israel! Who is like you, a people saved by the Lord? He is your shield and **helper** and your glorious sword...' " (**Deuteronomy 33:29**).

"May He send you **help** from the sanctuary and grant you support from Zion" (**Psalms 20:2**).

"We wait in hope for the Lord; He is our **help** and our shield" (**Psalms 33:20**).

"Yet I am poor and needy; come quickly to me, O God. You are my **help** and my deliverer; O Lord, do not delay" (**Psalms 70:5**).

"Then you spoke in a vision to your holy one, and said: 'I have given **help** to one who is mighty; I have exalted one chosen from the people' " (**Psalms 89:19** NKJV). The NIV says strength in place of help.

"O house of Israel, trust in the Lord— He is their **help** and shield. O house of Aaron, trust in the Lord— He is their **help** and shield. You who fear him, trust in the Lord— he is their **help** and shield" (**Psalm 115:9-11**).

"I lift up my eyes to the hills—where does my **help** come from? My **help** comes from the Lord, the Maker of heaven and earth " (**Psalm 121:1-2**).

"Our **help** is in the name of the Lord, the Maker of heaven and earth" (**Psalms 124:8**).

"Blessed is he whose **help** is the God of Jacob, whose hope is in the Lord his God..." (**Psalms 146:5**).

"Everyone will be put to shame because of a people useless to them, who bring neither **help** nor advantage, but only shame and disgrace" (**Isaiah 30:5**). Isaiah is telling the people of Jerusalem that Egypt will not be the kind of help that they need.

" 'I will scatter to every wind all who are around him to **help** him, and all his troops; and I will draw out the sword after them' " (**Ezekiel 12:14**). God is telling the people of Judah that he will put to flight those that Judah has called on to "help" them.

" 'When they fall, they will receive a little **help**, and many who are not sincere will join them" (**Daniel 11:34**).

" 'You are destroyed, O Israel, because you are against me, against your **helper**' " (**Hosea 13:9**).

If you will go back to Genesis, you will find there was no suitable helper for Adam among the beasts of the earth or the birds of the air. God had it in his heart to make a helper and made a woman. Now, if you looked seriously at the other verses that use the same word for help, you have discovered every verse refers to God being the help, or the fact that another country could not provide the kind of help that God can. When God made a "suitable helper" for Adam, what he made was a vessel by which he could give his help to Adam. As a woman, a wife, you will be the largest source of God's divine help in your husband's life. You were made a woman to be the means by which God could give man His help.

With that knowledge comes both encouragement and responsibility. We know that Egypt did not depict God's divine help to Judah. He called them weak and worthless. Ladies, if you will not allow God to use you for that which you were created, you are neglecting one of, if not the largest, job that God has given you to do. Let us give a deeper translation of those verses in Genesis. "God looked for a means by which He could give His supernatural help to Adam and there was none, so He made a way to give His supernatural help to Adam and it was Eve." Ladies, God created you to be a vessel of supernatural power and help. That should excite you! You have no idea what a great blessing you will be to your husband as you become everything God has made you to be.

SUBMITTING HELPER

"Wives, submit to your husbands as to the Lord. For the husband is the head of the wife as Christ is the head of the church, His body, of which He is the Savior" (**Ephesians 5:22,23**). I think both the over-bearing husband and the women-libber wife bend these verses out of shape. But these verses are not bad; it does not put the woman in a servant role. "Wives, submit to your husbands, as it is fitting in the Lord" (**Colossians 3:18**). "Now as the church submits to Christ, so also wives should submit to their husbands in everything" (**Ephesians 5:24**). Here is my thinking on this passage: Christ is the head of the church, which makes us the hands and feet of Christ. Though God is capable to run the whole show by himself, and bring people into a relationship with him, He opts to use us as vessels, as a means by which He is carried to others. Just as the hands and feet of our body cannot move without having been informed to do so by the brain, how do we as the church know what to do if not first told by Christ? More than just the head of me, Christ is my husband. He guides me and lets me know where to go and what to do. In the marriage relationship, the woman submits to her husband "as is fitting in the Lord." Obviously, you are not going to submit to the will of your husband when he tells you to run through the street in a chicken costume singing Yankee-Doodle-Dandy (I'm sorry, I could think of absolutely nothing else!). If your husband is serving God he will be the Spiritual leader. Hopefully he has your best interest at heart. But even if you are married to an ungodly man, the Bible gives direction to you to submit to him, as long as it is in keeping with the word of God (**1 Peter 3:1-7**). Still take note that before the woman is commanded to submit to her husband, we find that God commands that a couple "submit to one another in the fear of Christ." **Ephesians 5: 21.** Still if things are being done in a godly fashion it will not be harmful to the wife to submit to her husband.

SOMEONE WITH A TENDER TONGUE

James tells us we "should be quick to listen, slow to speak, and slow to become angry" (**James 1:19**). A wife also should have a slow tongue: "A quarrelsome wife is like a constant dripping" (**Proverbs 19:13**). Have you ever heard of Chinese water torture? The idea was they would restrain a prisoner they wanted to get information out of. They would then set the prisoner's head under a constant drip. At first the water would hit your head and you would hardly notice it, but after a long period of time, each drop feels like the stroke of a hammer. In nature, water dripping from a constant source cuts holes through stone. A quarrelsome wife is like a constant drip. When your husband, who is seeking God, is moving, you must not be quarrelsome. Imagine what it would have been like for Abram if Sarai had said, "God told you to go where? I'm not going." Or perhaps she goes, but all the while she is complaining about everything to bring Abram to a boil. We are told it is "better to live on a corner of the roof than share a house with a quarrelsome wife." It is even better to live in the desert than with her (**Proverbs 21:9,19**). Remind yourself to keep quiet a moment longer before you speak. Why should you always be a thorn in your husband's side? I don't mean to pick on the ladies, but it does seem that women have more of an issue with this than men. There are multiple commands to the woman throughout the Bible that she ought not be quarrelsome, or given over to gossip. So, ladies, be a delight to your husband by refusing to be quarrelsome. Be loving and kind in your speech. Let your words be a blessing and not a curse.

PRUDENT: WISE—DISCREET—FRUGAL

"Houses and wealth are inherited from parents, but a prudent wife is from the Lord" (**Proverbs 19:14**). How do you handle the things you are involved in? Do you have wisdom? Are you discreet when dealing with the things that are happening not only in the lives of your friends, but even more so in the dealings with your husband? Are you frugal in spending and saving money? I once heard a young woman who had just gotten married to a man about four or five years older than her recounting a story to a friend. She proudly told her friend how much she liked to spend money and how her husband had told her if she didn't start spending less money she would have to get a job. She boasted of the things she had just bought, and was particularly pleased with the expensive ring she had bought herself for Christmas. The ring, of course, was from her husband—after she informed him she bought it. I cringe to think of what home must be like for that couple. Handle the things in your household with discretion, with wisdom, and with prudence. Be wise about what you say in public. Be discreet in your dress. Be wise in how you handle yourself. There is much more to say about this so let's look at Proverbs 31.

A WIFE OF NOBLE CHARACTER

It is evident upon a reading of the epilogue in Proverbs 31, what a woman seeking God would look like. I have sought to understand what this passage might teach me. (Obviously not because I want to be a "wife of noble character," or as another translation heads this passage, "a worthy woman," but because I was curious to find what I may learn about the type of wife I should seek out.) While King Lemuel puts down on paper many great qualities of a woman, his overall feeling can be summed up in the first verse of this particular passage. "A wife of noble character who can find? She is worth far more than rubies" (**Proverbs 31:10**). The following verses go into the diligence she puts forth in the work she does. I will not take the time now to type out all 22 verses, but I do want you to take the time to read the passage in its entirety (verses 10-31). In my having prayerfully considered this text, there are, I think, fourteen things I have come to look for in a wife. While I do not expect these fourteen things to be exclusive, I do hope they will offer some insight to both the man and the woman reading this now.

- "The heart of her husband trusts in her, and he will have no lack of gain" (**Pr. 31:11** NAS). What a thing it is to trust in someone; to know they have your best interests in mind. To know that there is no deceptive speech in her mouth. How wonderful it is to know that even in your absence, someone has regard for your character and your business, your very life. It is no wonder the husband will have no lack of gain. He is married to a trustworthy woman.
- "She does him good and not evil all the days of her life" (**Pr. 31:12** NAS). If you will indulge me for a moment, I may expound with greater detail what I believe to be the definition of the word "good;" I think you will find this particular verse quite striking. **James 1:17** tells us that "every good and perfect gift comes down from the father of heavenly lights." In **Matthew 19:17**, Christ indicates there is no one good but

165

God. Think on this for a moment. If there is nothing good but that which comes from God, then for this verse to say, "She does him good and not evil" is to say his wife treats him in a godly manner. A godly manner! Not only does she do this, but she does it with persistence and consistency all the days of her life! What a wonderful trait.

- "She looks for wool and flax, and works with her hands in delight (willingly)" (**Pr. 31:13** NAS). Here we see that she is a woman who will work with joy, not only joy, but in a willful manner. What a treasure to have a wife as a willing worker! One who will look diligently to those things that God has set before her.

- "She rises while it is still night, and gives food to her household, and portions to her maidens" (**Pr. 31:15** NAS). I think it is clear to see she is a woman set on meeting the needs of those under the authority of her household. Notice her concern does not end with her family, but extends to those who share her roof as well.

- "She considers a field and buys it; from the fruit of her palms (her earnings) she plants a vineyard" (**Pr. 31:16** NAS). This woman is wise and uses that wisdom to consider how she might bless the family. Notice she takes some of her own money and, with consideration, purchases a field so she can plant a vineyard. A woman who will not only show wisdom, but also consideration and discretion in her spending is a worthy woman indeed.

- "She girds herself with strength, and makes her arms strong" (**Pr. 31:17** NAS). While there is something to be said about the dependence a wife will have on her husband, and while there is a very valid need in a God-minded marriage for the husband to nurture his wife, there is no reason that the wife would not pursue strength. I do not mean to imply physical strength, but that she should pursue the independence and freedom afforded to her under Christ Jesus. Truly a well rounded woman is one who can be nurtured and cared for by her husband, while standing strong on her own in Christ.

- "Her lamp does not go out at night" (**Pr. 31:18** NAS). I think this simply is to say she is always prepared. Always ready for whatever may be required of her.

- "She extends her hand to the poor; and stretches out her hands to the needy" (**Pr. 31:20** NAS). Obviously, she is a woman who is dedicated to meeting the needs of others. Not only those under her own household, but the needs of whomever she may come in contact with.

- "She is not afraid of the snow for her household, for all her household are clothed with scarlet" (**Pr. 31:21** NAS). If we look carefully to why this wife is not fearful, it is because her family is well cared for. True that a godly woman has her mind set on God, but a woman whose mind is set on God yet her obediences are not, will be a woman of fear. This woman is free from fear because her heart is set on

God primarily, but also because she has been obedient to look after the needs of her family as He has directed.

- "Her husband is respected at the city gate, where he takes his seat among the elders of the land" (**Pr. 31:23** NAS). I was puzzled by this; why is a verse about her husband mixed in with the epilogue? Isn't this supposed to be about a wife of noble character? Then why this interjection about her husband? Then it hit me! "A wife of noble character is her husband's crown" (**Proverbs 12:4**). You see, though I cannot explain how it works for sure, it is evident that a wife of noble character affects the way others look at the husband. You as a wife will, to a large degree, be responsible for the way that others view your mate. It is a big responsibility, but one you should set out to complete with rejoicing. Who should want more for your husband to be well thought of than you? So this verse simply indicates that because of how she speaks of her husband in public, he is well respected. Wives, be sure that you are careful to make sure that your husband is well respected in the city gates. You will do so by being a beautiful crown on his head and by guarding fiercely how others see him.

- "Strength and dignity are her clothing, and she smiles at the future (latter days)" (**Pr. 31:25** NAS). We have already touched on the strength of a wife of noble character, and we can understand she can smile at the future for her lack of fear; but notice here it says she is also clothed with dignity. She is noble, or has about her the air of nobility. She is discreet and cautious and gentle and tender. Further, I think dignity implies confidence. This too comes from the knowledge of who she is in Jesus and before God by the Holy Spirit, and can only add to the marriage relationship.

- "She opens her mouth in wisdom, and the teaching (law) of kindness is on her tongue" (**Pr. 31:26** NAS). If I were to be honest, I would have to say there is listed among the characteristics of a worthy woman many terrific qualities, all of which are imperative to the health of a marriage and all of which I would desire in a wife, but this one is perhaps one of my favorites. A woman who opens her mouth in wisdom is most assuredly a woman whose mouth has been filled with wisdom. God tells us to "open your mouth wide and I will fill it" (**Ps. 81:10** NAS). This speaks to many things; not least among them is wisdom. Further, we know "the mouth speaks out of that which fills the heart" (**Mt. 12:34** NAS). This indicates a woman who speaks wisdom and is filled to the fullest with it. There is nothing more beautiful to me than a woman who can speak in the wisdom of God. There is nothing more attractive than one who has God's wisdom tightly wound up in her heart. Not to be odious or offensive, but in light of all I have just said, I must agree with

King Lemuel and say, "An excellent wife, who can find?"

- "She looks well to the ways of her household, and does not eat the bread of idleness" (**Pr. 31:27** NAS). Simply put, she is not lazy.
- "Charm is deceitful and beauty is vain, but a woman who fears the LORD, she shall be praised" (**Pr. 31:30** NAS). This is easily my second favorite. I think it only appropriate to sum up all of the previous characteristics with this one. Truly if a woman fears the LORD, then all these others will be in place.

As women, may your prayer be to resemble this pattern; as men, may you seek this out in your spouse. May the Lord bless you both in these pursuits. I will say that on reading this list again I can see how hard it is to find a wife of noble character. Many women are so far from these characteristics that it is near impossible to find one who has even half of them. But don't get mad, ladies, and don't get proud, men, for I could say that when we look in a moment at what a husband ought to be it is evident that few if any measure up to their calling in Christ.

WOMAN OF CONSTRUCTION

"The wise woman builds her house, but with her own hand the foolish one tears hers down" (**Proverbs 14:1**). Be a woman resolved to build up her house! We see in this verse that with your own hands you can tear down your house. Choose now to establish your house securely. Be a woman who is wise. "Fear of the Lord teaches wisdom, and humility comes before honor" (**Proverbs 15:33**). Remember ladies that you are the primary means by which God will give His divine help. In giving it, you will build your home up into holiness and in withholding it, you will certainly see your home destroyed.

A HUSBAND LIKE CHRIST
4-14-03
My Sweet Wife, (wherever you are)

I just want you to know that with all of my heart I want to be a husband who loves you in the same manner that Christ loved the church. With all of my heart I will lay down my life for yours and I will serve you daily with all devotion. I will seek to make you famous and to build a home for us that exemplifies the strength of our relationship with Christ. I will cherish you and honor you above all else. I have been enthusiastically seeking the day you would be a part of my life. I love you and am praying for you.

ryan

Men, we are called to resemble Christ. As He is our husband and we His bride, we have a perfect example of how to treat our suitable helper. "Husbands, love your wives, just as Christ loved the church and gave Himself up for her…" (**Ephesians 5:25**). Though we have already covered this, I want to mention just once more that you are the lover in the relationship. If you ever have any doubt about how to properly love your bride, simply ask yourself "how does Christ love me", and do what He would do. You are His bride and He has loved you perfectly. Resolve now to love her such that you have given yourself up for her. Christ went to the cross that we would not have to. Love your bride. "Under three things the earth trembles, under four it cannot bear up: ...an unloved woman who is married" (**Proverbs 30:21,23**). The earth trembles under the weight of a married woman who isn't loved rightly!

This concept of loving your bride like Christ loved the church isn't just some nice idea that Paul mentions in passing; this is Scripture. This is true and right and good. Men, if you do not love your wife like Christ has loved you, you are wrong! It is not ok to be "kinda doing it", nor learning about it, nor trying. You must be like Christ toward your wife! Now granted, you will try and you will still be learning about it, but to whatever degree God has revealed Himself to you, to that degree should you be practicing the Christ-like love of your wife. How was it that Christ behaved? Christ was *gentle*, and able to *meet needs*, and a *teacher* and a *helper*, and *always willing* to be of some assistance *even when He was tired* or trying to have time alone. He *never abandoned* anyone, *never spoke anything but the truth*, *never misstated His purpose or intentions*, *never avoided someone who was seeking Him out*. He was *always submissive to God*, *always sought God in prayer*, and was faithful to *continually give credit to God*. He *always blessed*, and *gave edification*, He always *sought to heal* those who were wounded. He would *stay up late, and rise early to accomplish time with God*. He was a *leader*, He had *confidence*, and He always *took the time to listen* to someone's voice. He would *rebuke* that some might come nearer God.

- Gentle- So then, be gentle with your wife in speech and action.
- Meet needs- Meet the needs your wife has told you about and those you happen to notice on your own.
- Teacher- Take your wife to the Bible on a regular basis that you may instruct her in the things of God.
- Helper- Never be too important to help your wife with the dishes, picking out a pattern of dinnerware, the yard, the kids, a crisis, whatever.
- Always willing- Be always willing to be near your wife in a helpful way. Not grudgingly willing, but really willing. Whether you are tired or had already made other plans. Your wife is your flesh; tend to it. After God, she comes first. Not golf, not sleep, not "time with the guys."
- Never abandon- Don't even say you will; don't say it in anger or in jest. It is a terribly wicked jest at best, deserving the wrath of God. Abandonment and the fear of it will destroy. Never, ever abandon. Don't even sleep on the couch; this is to abandon her in bed. Don't leave the house in the midst of conflict; this is to abandon her in storm. Never abandon her.

Not for your work; not for things. Never ever abandon!!!

- Speak truth- Without exception, speak truth. Do not exaggerate, do not lie (by the way, exaggeration is a lie). Never tell her you're in a meeting when you aren't. Don't deceive on any level. Never give the opportunity to question your speech. It will devastate her to think you have lied. It will destroy you both if you do.

- Always be honest in purpose and intentions- you may think I take this too far, but I don't even care for surprise parties. They involve way too much deceit in their initial stages. You come home late from the office because you had a meeting with her best friend to plan your wife's party. When your wife asks why you were late you lie or avoid the question. Over the next few weeks you build doubt and distrust into the relationship. Trust me, it's not worth it. Tell her up front "Hey, the next few weeks I'll be planning your surprise party so I might be home a bit late from work or have some private phone calls." Again, you may think that I am taking this too far but if your wife grew up in a home where one of her parents were unfaithful, I can promise you that you don't want to do anything that nurtures distrust or suspicion. When you come to your wife with something to say, speak it clearly and directly without beating around the bush.

- Never avoid someone seeking you- This is not abandonment; this is avoiding. While they both start with "a," they are different in act, yet similar in response. A woman avoided will conjure up "secrets" you are keeping. Perhaps true, perhaps deceptions of Satan. Further, you will cripple her self-worth as a wife. Rather, if your wife is seeking you, you should respond by hastening to her. When was God sought that He would not draw Himself near? **Jeremiah 29:12,13**

- Submissive to God- If you are not submissive to God, you have nothing. You do not know what it means to be a husband or even a man. You are a child lost in futile ways of thinking and are guilty of indulging yourself in the world. Be submissive to Him in EVERYTHING!

- Seek God in prayer- **1 Thessalonians 5:16—** Prayer is vital to your role as a husband and a believer in Christ. Communicate with God Almighty on every matter. In all things, seek the counsel of God.

- Give God the credit- Every good thing in your life has come from Him and is His, so give Him the credit due.

- Always blessing- You are to bless your wife daily. Bless her with your words and your actions. Surprise her with your blessings until she is no longer surprised and knows they will come because they are stored in your heart for her, just as in the heart of God are many blessings for us.

- Edify- Encourage your wife. Tell her how great she is and how fantastic she looks and encourage her to be more Christ-minded and love her that way.
- Seek to heal the wounded- We have covered this already in the section on "one flesh," but let me say it again: make it an urgent priority to heal your wife's wounds. And as often as they need to be dressed and treated, treat her until she is well.
- Stay up late/rise early for time with God- Invest your time in God. Make Him "IT" in your life. In that, all other things will be tended to as needed. If you must get up early or stay up late to be with God, do it! If you don't have time with God, you are wrong.
- Leadership- Lead your wife. Take responsibility for her.
- Confidence- Be confident in who you are in Christ. Your wife needs to see that. It will bless her and reassure her. It will also help her recognize you as a leader.
- Listen- Never underestimate the importance of listening. I know as a guy you always want to give advice or fix the problem, there will be a time and a place for that. Christ always attended to the need, but first, He would listen.
- Rebuke- Rebuke your wife. God rebukes us. Do it gently and Biblically-backed. Never offer a rebuke that is your opinion; be certain if you do, you are likely sinning against her and God.

Take her to Scripture on the issues. This is right. Let me say again, do it gently.

MAN WHO CHERISHES

"For no one ever hated his own flesh, but nourishes and cherishes it, just as Christ also does the church, because we are members of His body" (**Ephesians 5:29-30** NAS). Again, we have here the idea of "one flesh." As I consider what I want to say in this section, I cannot help but smile and, at the same time, be a bit grieved. I smile because to cherish someone is grand, and I am grieved because I once cherished someone and she is gone. Still, the grief can't remain; she is gone and was never to be cherished by me in the manner my wife shall one day be cherished. A man can cherish the way his wife smells, or looks, or touches him. He can appreciate the way she will step right in to his body and hold him tight, and how his chin rests on her head, as he catches the fragrance of her hair. He can cherish that her touch is so gentle he has to open his eyes to see if it's really there. He can cherish her kiss, that she would gently lay her lips on him, even if it were only on his hand. He can cherish her voice, her singing, her smile. But a man who cherishes, must be one who lets his wife know he cherishes her. Spend time with her; give her flowers. Read to her sweet poetry. Dance with her when no one is looking and when everyone is. Kiss her softly on the mouth and tell her how much she means to you. Men, be tender with your wife. Be gentle. Be like a whisper to her heart and like sun on her face. Invest time in her. Cradle her always in your heart.

Never let that escape; never let it mellow with time. I write this section with tears in my eyes, for I know truly how great it is to cherish things about someone, and to be able to cherish someone in what we do and say. And I long for my wife that I may cherish her daily. Ladies, never marry a man who does not cherish you. This is a most blessed attribute. A most honored gift. Oh, how a heart longs to cherish and be cherished! Resolve yourself, men, to do this without bias, without hesitation. Cherish your wife!

MAN OF CONSTRUCTION

"The beams of our house are cedars; our rafters are firs" (**Song of Solomon 1:17**). Begin before the wedding to make your house a strong one. If the wife is able to build a house, it is your job to make sure it's solid and strong. What is so interesting about this verse is that it was written before the wedding. Before you are ever married, your house should be strong. "But whoever listens to me will live in safety and be at ease…" (**Proverbs 1:33**). "Therefore, everyone who hears these words of mine and puts them into practice is like a wise man who built his house on the rock. The rain came down, the streams rose, and the winds blew and beat against that house; yet it did not fall, because it had its foundation on the rock" (**Matthew 7:24, 25**). A strong house is not determined by where you live, whether if it's an apartment, trailer, or made of brick or wood. A strong house is determined by how much God is allowed there. You husbands will make a strong home when you submit to God. Men, listen to God, and build your house on "nothing less than Jesus' blood and righteousness."

THE ONE WHO WASHES

"Husbands, love your wives, just as Christ loved the church and gave Himself up for her to make her holy, cleansing her by the washing with water through the word..." (**Ephesians 5:25,26**).

"Sanctify them by Your truth. Your word is truth" (**John 17:17**). There is no question in my mind that this is one of the most important duties you have to your wife. Just because she has her own time with God does not give you a right to neglect her. You must share God with your wife. Not in the sense that you would with someone who does not know God, but in the sense that you continue sharpening her; you continue preparing her for God. Does not the Bible promise that, "The God of peace will sanctify you through and through...to be kept blameless at the coming of our Lord Jesus Christ" (**1 Thessalonians 5:23**). Men, take great pleasure and joy in loving your wife in a relationship with God Almighty! Rejoice as you share with her God and His truths! God rejoices in heaven as the Spirit counsels you and forms you to resemble Christ. Men, rejoice as your wife resembles Christ. Do not let her do it alone. Take her to Christ; lead her there in the Bible, in prayer, in serving, and in ministering before the Faithful God. Yet remember, if you are going to lead and sharpen her, then you must know God and be sharp yourself. Do not neglect to worship before God in your study of Him and His truths. Talk to Him so that you might be a proper example. What an awesome responsibility! What a joyous one!

ONE WHO BRINGS FAME

Remember when we talked about Song of Songs 4: 4? "Your neck is like the tower of David, built with elegance; on it hang a thousand shields, all of them shields of warriors." In Ezekiel, when he was prophesying against Tyre, he spoke of how popular they were. "Those of Persia, Lydia, and Libya were in your army as men of war; they hung shield and helmet in you; they gave splendor to you. Men of Arvad with your army were on your walls all around, and the men of Gammad were in your towers; they hung their shields on your walls all around; they made your beauty perfect" (**Ezekiel 27:10, 11**). Tyre was so popular and well known that all that came to visit its halls would leave behind a shield or helmet and hang them on the walls to make Tyre perfect in beauty. In a similar way, when God tells the allegory of having found Israel in a field as a baby and raising it to be His bride, He says, "Your fame went out among the nations because of your beauty, for it was perfect through My splendor which I have bestowed upon you" (**Ezekiel 16:14**). All this to say that just as the wife is responsible for how her husband will be viewed, so it is up to the husband to build for his wife a position of fame and standing among all people. It is the husband's role to see his wife is thought well of and revered far and wide. Most often when men mention their wives publicly it is derogatory or insulting. Let other men hear you speak highly of your wife. Exalt her in public. Praise her and highly esteem her that her fame may go throughout the earth.

MAN OF HONOR

"Husbands, in the same way, be considerate as you live with your wives, and treat them with respect as the weaker partner and as heirs with you of the gracious gift of life, so that nothing will hinder your prayers" (**1 Peter 3:7**). Men, remember your wife was first your sister in Christ. She is heir to all you are heir to. That means that all you are in Christ she is also. Never forget the good you do is by God and the good she does is by God. You will both, as Christians, receive eternity with God and the power of the Spirit. Be considerate of her always and honor her, because she too is a vessel of God and His most holy temple (**1 Corinthians 6:19**).

CHAPTER SIXTEEN
PAUL WAS WEIRD! (okay, not really)

I have often been puzzled by Paul's view of marriage. He tells everyone in **1 Corinthians 7**, he wishes they were as he is.

> "I would like you to be free from concern. An unmarried man is concerned about the Lord's affairs—how he can please the Lord. But a married man is concerned about the affairs of this world—how he can please his wife—and his interests are divided. An unmarried woman or virgin is concerned about he Lord's affairs: Her aim is to be devoted to the Lord in both body and spirit. But a married woman is concerned about the affairs of this world—how she can please her husband. I am saying this for your own good, not to restrict you, but that you may live in a right way in undi-

vided devotion to the Lord." (**1 Corinthians 7:32-35**)

This is what I know to be true: married and single people alike have the opportunity to know God and to know him well. There is potential for both the married and unmarried to know God equally well, but the danger is that the married person will be distracted. Let me tell you what to look for in a marriage relationship, and how to protect yourself from the distraction of a spouse.

First of all, it is good to know when someone loves you correctly you will begin to understand and know God better. In a marriage relationship this is only intensified. As your spouse pours out upon your life the love of God, you understand better how it is that God loves you and you begin to grow and change. Out of all the Israelites that left Egypt, only Moses was invited upon the mountain to receive the law of God. There is no doubt, though, that when he came down from the mountain he was able to teach the law to the others there. As a result of Moses showing them the law of God, the people of the land came to a better understanding of who God was. Yet only one man had gone up to the mountain. The priests served before God in the temple and in the Holy of Holies and offered sacrifices there. As a result of the work of the priests, the people of Israel came to understand and to know God more completely. But only the priests served before God in the temple. You see, we are to come to know God better as a result of the people in our lives that are serving Him, but it is when we rely solely on those individuals to show us God that we become distracted. With the death of Christ, all of us were allowed into the Holy of Holies. It has been made available for all of us to seek and find God on our own. We no longer need a middleman to serve as an interpreter between Him and us. Your spouse will become the distraction, will hinder the way you are seeing God, when you set up between you and Him an individual as a priest. God has invited you to fellowship before Him, so go and do this without hesitation. I am not against listening to pastors or being sharpened in your faith by a faithful follower of God; I am, however, reminding you to never fail to seek Him on your own.

I believe Paul knew the temptation was for the married individual to look more to their spouse for the things of God than to God. Also, Paul was probably aware that when one with strong faith in God is joined to one with small faith, the results are often disastrous. After all, the one with strong faith will more often stumble and be found weaker because of his/her partner, rather than the other way around. I once had a friend caution me in this regard. I suppose he has been married nearly twenty years, but as we were talking, he shared the importance of marrying one who is on equal ground with you spiritually. He confessed when he had married his wife, she was not spiritually stable and caused him to digress in his spiritual life for the better part of three years. Now his wife serves alongside him and is a godly woman, yet he recognizes how devastating to his own spiritual growth the initial years had been. Therefore, seek God and He will be found by you.

The most obvious way that a spouse will distract you in your service of God is that you will be so concerned for their wellbeing that you will be likely to turn aside from the difficult things God has told you to do. When we are single we are more free in our decision making process since it bears consequences for us alone. But when we are married now all of our decisions have the power to not only hurt us but also our spouse and where we would have once run fearlessly after God we now pause and hesitate in our obedience. There is no avoiding the fact that a spouse will distract you, but that is all the more reason to be sure you are going to marry a godly person.

That we might have an even greater understanding of what Paul was talking about, let us look to the first part of this same chapter:

"Now concerning the things about which you wrote, it is good for a man not to touch a woman. But because of immoralities, let each man have his own wife, and let each woman have her own husband. Let the husband fulfill his duty to his wife, and likewise also the wife to her husband. The wife does not have authority over her own body, but the husband does; and likewise also the husband does not have authority over his own body, but the wife does. Stop depriving one another, except by agreement for a time that you may devote yourselves to prayer, and come together again

lest Satan tempt you because of your lack of self-control. But this I say by way of concession, not of command. Yet I wish that all men were even as I myself am. However, each man has his own gift from God, one in this manner, and another in that. But I say to the unmarried and to the widows that it is good for them if they remain even as I. But if they do not have self-control, let them marry; for it is better to marry than to burn with passion."
1 Corinthians 7:1-9

There are three places in this short text where Paul makes mention to sexual immorality. Perhaps the reason is simply because these nine verses deal almost exclusively with the physical relationship and the desires therein. In verse two, he comments that since there are immoralities, each man should take a wife, and each woman a husband. In verse five, he speaks of the sexual temptation that comes when a husband and wife have consented to put aside sexual intercourse for the benefit of prayer. Finally, Paul alludes to sexual impurity in verse nine; indicating it is better to marry than to burn with passion.

In the first case, it is merely factual information. Paul is saying because there are immoralities among men, each should take a spouse. It makes sense; Paul has just finished declaring that sexual sins are against the body while all others are outside the body, and we are to glorify God in our bodies (**1 Corinthians 6:18,20**). In his next written word, he declares it is best for men not to touch women. Notice also he is responding to what they had written him about; no doubt this church is dealing with sexual desires and temptations at every turn. Paul tells them not to even touch each other. I almost agree with him here. How many times has a touch or a kiss birthed in my heart unholy passions? Still, Paul seems to know that immoralities are pressing hard upon this group of believers seeking to honor God, so he instructs them to marry.

Notice, though, that marriage is not the end to the problematic issues of unholy sexual desire (there is holy sexual desire by the way; it is between a man and his wife alone). Paul says that because the man's body doesn't belong to him but to his wife, and because the wife's body doesn't belong to her but her husband, they are not to deprive each other. Paul is speaking of sex. Basically he says that "I have a headache," or "just another nine holes then I'll be home," must be thrown out. A man and wife are encouraged to be sexual with each other. Paul says the only reason you may not have sex is so you may devote yourself to some matter in prayer together. Yet he cautions the married couple not to go on too long in this manner, lest they be tempted away by their lack of self-control. Now, do not think in all this Paul is throwing up his hands and saying there is no hope for sexual purity. Do not think Paul is saying that lacking self-control is ok or expected. Remember that the fruit of the Spirit includes self-control (**Galatians 5:22-23**). We are to demonstrate self-control. But we further know we are not tempted until we are dragged away by our own evil desires and enticed (**James 1:14**). So in all of this, Paul is simply cautioning the married couple (who have every right to desire sex) that they ought not to abstain too long, lest those same desires be turned to other places.

In verse nine, having just said how it is better to stay unmarried, Paul again emphasizes if those who are single "do not have self-control," they should marry. He tells us it is better to be married than to burn with those passions. Again, do not assume that demonstrations of lack of self-control are ok. We are called, and commanded, to be holy and to possess ourselves in self-control. I am of the firm opinion that the most blessed marriage and marriage bed are the ones entered into where each partner had control of their bodies and lived lives of self-control.

One other note on this passage: in verse four, it notes the body of the husband does not belong to him, but to his wife, and the body of the wife belongs to her husband; I think we can find one other truth that advocates the single life. Notice it says the man has no authority over his own body or the wife hers. It's that word authority. When we are married we are accountable to our spouse with where our body is and what it does. Remember the body is not ours any longer. As a single minister, I have an incredible advantage to the married man. My body is under no one's authority but God's. I have the freedom to plan mission trips, retreats, camps, and many other minis-terial opportunities without checking with anybody. I am not a cynic; if I were married, I would be so gladly. Yet as a married man I would, by obligation of Scripture and my own personal convictions, be unable to plan out-of-town trips, camps, or the like without first asking my wife; without first seeing if she needs me, or if she can go with me, or if we have prior engagements. Truly, there are advantages to being accountable to none but God in our bodies.

Let me throw out another thought. Let us look one more time at what Paul says in **1 Corinthians 7:4:** "The wife does not have authority over her own body, but the husband does; and likewise also the husband does not have authority over his own body, but the wife does." Notice it does not say to the husband, "you have authority over your wife's body," nor does it say to the wife, "you have authority over your husband's body." What it does say to the wife is that her body isn't her own, but her husband's, and to the husband that his body isn't his, but his wife's. You may think there is no difference in those statements, but there is. The way Paul phrases this signifies not a matter of possession but, rather, a lack of possession. In our day and age we want to make everything about what we want or have or are chasing. Paul doesn't say to the husband, "I want you to know that your wife's body isn't hers but it is yours." Instead, he says to the wife, "I want you to know that your body isn't yours but belongs to your husband." The difference, though subtle, is that the first emphasizes the possession of the husband, while the second emphasizes the service or servant attitude of the wife. In a marriage relationship, it shouldn't be about "the Bible says your body is mine, so here is what I want you to do…" It should be about "the Bible says my body isn't mine, so how can I serve you?" Let me try to say this one more time and perhaps more plainly. When I get married God's word to me is that my body isn't my own anymore but that it belongs to my wife, which actually makes me her servant. The command of God to my future wife is that her body isn't hers anymore but that it belongs to me, thus making her my servant. So then the husband is instructed to serve the wife and the wife is instructed to serve the husband. We are not to take from this verse that the husband is the boss of the wife's body and with wife is the boss of the husband's body. That would be a terrible abuse of the text. If we would get that down, that we are to serve one another in marriage, our marriages wouldn't be ending 54% of the time. Remember love is not self-seeking, so your attitude should not be "your body is mine," but "my body is yours." Seek to make it so in your marriage.

CHAPTER SEVENTEEN

THE CALL TO BE SINGLE

The question undoubtedly arises in the heart: is there such a thing as the call to be single? Before I answer that question, let me say both of the men in the New Testament who taught on marriage believed it to be acceptable, if not beneficial, to be single. We have looked at Paul; the other is Christ. "Not all men can accept this statement, but only those to whom it **has been given**. For there are eunuchs who were born that way from their mother's womb; and eunuchs who were made eunuchs by men; and there are also eunuchs who made themselves eunuchs for the sake of the kingdom of heaven. He who is able to accept this, let him accept it" (**Matthew 19:11-12** NAS). A eunuch was an emasculated man; one who was set aside to serve queens or work with women, but not desire them. Now when Christ says "to him who is able, let him accept it," He is not saying men everywhere should take up the knife and do home surgery. He is saying, however, that those who can be single for the sake of the kingdom of heaven should be. I pose the question again. Is there such a thing as the call to be single? Absolutely! I am of the firm opinion at one point or another in everyone's life, all are called to be single. Think about it. I am single right now; if God wanted me married I would be. Apparently right now, I am to accept being single. Not a hard concept. Now as far as being single indefinitely, if you can accept it, do. If you can be single for the sake of the kingdom of heaven, do it. This means that you will not say, "I could be single but...." For one who could always be single, there is no "but." God prepares the one He calls to be single to be able to be single. There will not be the need to marry that others seem to feel so strongly. But notice also that Christ said only those to whom it has been given could accept this teaching. Further, Paul in **1 Corinthians 7** said each has his gift (**1 Corinthians 7:7**), implying simply that there are some to be married and some not. Still, as long as God allows for us to be single, let us accept that teaching as right for our life. But know also that the life of the eunuch is not one to be frowned upon; rather, that life receives great reward from God in eternity.

THE BLESSING OF THE EUNUCH

"Let not the foreigner who has joined himself to the Lord say, 'The Lord will surely separate me from His people.' Neither let the eunuch say, 'Behold, I am a dry tree.' For thus says the Lord, 'To the eunuchs who keep My Sabbaths, and choose what pleases Me, and hold fast My covenant, to them I will give in My house and within My walls a memorial, and a name better than that of sons and daughters; I will give them an everlasting name which will not be cut off." **Isaiah 56:3-5**

"And they sang a new song before the throne and before the four living creatures and the elders; and no one could learn the song except the one hundred and forty-four thousand who had been purchased from earth. These are the ones who have not been defiled with women, for they have kept themselves chaste. These are the ones who follow the Lamb wherever He goes. These have been purchased from among men as first fruits to God and to the Lamb. And no lie was found in their mouth; they are blameless." **Revelation 14:3-5**

The eunuch—those who have kept themselves pure from women—who obeys God by keeping His Sabbaths, choosing what pleases Him, and holding fast to His covenants, will have a name and a memorial, which is better than that of children he might have had. While this life may seem unappealing to us, there are great spiritual blessings in store for him who can "accept it."

CHAPTER EIGHTEEN

OH! THAT'S WHAT WE'RE DOING THIS FOR!

WHY DON'T WE LOVE

There are two reasons that we do not love the way the Bible has instructed us to. First, we fail to love correctly because we do not know what it looks like. We do not love because we are ignorant of what it is. However, now that you have seen what the Bible says as truth, you can no longer sin out of ignorance.

Second, we do not love because even though we know what it looks like, we just do not care to serve God obediently. We are in active rebellion.

You may be sinning out of ignorance, or you may be sinning out of disregard for the laws of God. Both of these reasons are sinful and are harmful to your relationship with the living God. If you do not know what to do, learn! If you know, then put those things into practice.

THE WORK OF LOVE IN THE LIVES OF THE GODLY

All this perhaps begs the question, "Why is it important to know all of this?" Perhaps you see the answer as obvious in your reading or studying of these notes. I would like to try to offer a little insight as to why I believe it is important that we not only know love, but that we understand it and live it.

"…So that Christ may dwell in your hearts through faith; and that you, being rooted and grounded in love, may be able to comprehend with all the saints what is the breadth and length and height and depth, and to know the love of Christ which surpasses knowledge, that you may be filled up to all the fullness of God" (**Ephesians 3:17-19**).

"And this I pray, that your love may abound still more and more in real knowledge and all discernment, so that you may approve the things that are excellent, in order to be sincere and blameless until the day of Christ; having been filled with the fruit of righteousness which comes through Jesus Christ, to the glory and praise of God" (**Philippians 1:9-11**).

"And so, as those who have been chosen of God, holy and beloved, put on a heart of compassion, kindness, humility, gentleness and patience; bearing with one another, and forgiving each other. Whoever has a complaint against anyone, just as the Lord forgave you, so also should you. And beyond all these things put on love, which is the uniting bond of perfectness" (**Colossians 3:12-14**).

"There is no fear in love; but perfect love casts out fear, because fear involves punishment, and the one who fears is not perfected in love" (**1 John 4:18**).

"Owe nothing to anyone except to love one another; for he who loves his neighbor has fulfilled the law. For this, 'You shall not commit adultery, you shall not murder, you shall not steal, you shall not covet,' and if there is any other commandment, it is summed up in this saying, 'you shall love your neighbor as yourself.' Love does no wrong to a neighbor; love therefore is the fulfillment of the law" (**Romans 13:8-10**).

"I am the LORD your God. Consecrate yourselves therefore, and be holy; for I am holy.... Thus you shall be holy for I am holy" (**Leviticus 11:44,45**).

God's desire for us has always been to be holy even as He is holy. He has made a way for us to achieve that through Christ Jesus and His love for us. Look at these few verses I have given you and realize they are a reoccurring theme throughout Scripture. As you come to know the length and depth and height and width of the love of God, as that knowledge fills your mind and heart, so shall you be filled with the very fullness of God. When your love abounds in knowledge and real discernment, you will "approve the things that are excellent, in order to be sincere and blameless," so that you will be "filled with the fruit of righteousness which comes through Jesus Christ." By these things you will give both glory and praise to God. Since you are commanded to put on things like compassion, humility, kindness, and gentleness, it is good to know love; love is what binds these things together in perfect unity. If the Bible teaches that one who fears has not been made perfect in love, it stands to reason that it is possible to be made perfect in love. I think at this point I want to interject what could be another book of its own, but I will try to limit it to a few lines. When we receive Christ as Lord and Savior of our lives, we are, in the eyes of God, perfect in holiness and righteousness (**Ephesians 4:22-24**). This is our standing before Him. Our conduct before Him, however, will change and improve as we better understand this love He has given us. We see how Paul's letter to the Romans teaches us that love is the fulfillment of the law. If this is indeed true, and I know it to be, a perfect understanding of love enables us to live in a holy way as God has called us to live; in that perfect, whole understanding we will fulfill the Law. What a tremendous and beautiful gift God has given us in love. He loves us. We learn to love others. We apply what we learn to our relationships with strangers, friends, enemies, and spouses, and the final result is that we learn to be holy even as our God is holy!

CHAPTER NINETEEN

LET SLEEPING DOGS LIE OR THEY MAY BITE YOU

DO NOT AROUSE OR WAKEN LOVE UNTIL...

Previous pages having been spent explaining what love should look like and how we should honor a prospective—or an actual—mate, and I am now compelled to admonish those among us who are single. By single, I mean not married and thereby include casual daters, exclusive daters, and the engaged in this grouping. This section is particularly hard for me to write as it speaks directly to the very source of pride and impatience in my life. You will remember that "love is patient," and if impatience enters into even our pursuit of love certainly we are not lovers as we ought to be, even if we have not yet had the chance to be actual lovers. Let me show you three other verses which we have previously ignored in Song of Songs.

"**I adjure you**, O daughters of Jerusalem, by the gazelles or by the hinds of the field, **that you will not arouse or awaken my love, until she [or it] pleases**" (**Song of Songs 2:7**).

"**I adjure you**, O daughters of Jerusalem, by the gazelles or by the hinds of the field**, that you will not arouse or awaken my love, until she [or it] pleases.**" (**Song of Songs 3:5**).

"**I want you to swear**, O daughters of Jerusalem, **do not arouse or awaken my love, until she [or it] pleases**" (**Song of Songs 8:4**).

How unfortunate it is for us who have sojourned long in our singlehood that this thought, this warning, this admonition is in the Bible, and not only is it there, but it occurs three times. Not only does it occur three times, but also it occurs in the book of the Bible that is the champion of love and romance. Three times in the book that stirs the heart of the single (and hopefully keeps lit the heart of the married) is this almost grotesque statement—or is it a command?—"do not arouse or awaken love until she pleases." You are wondering why I called the statement "grotesque," aren't you? It is quite simple; I have been a pilgrim upon this earth for very nearly thirty years. Actually, seven years ago when I was just 22 I started this project, but can you imagine it took me until now to grab hold of these three verses? These verses are grotesque to me because everything in my single little heart desires the love of a wife. Everything in my single little head believes I deserve as much. Pride creeps in and begins to proclaim loudly in my

202

ear, "it's past time for you to have this love. You can make it work. Find her. You deserve her." And I listen and believe this proud whisper. Suddenly, impatience floods my heart and I feel anxious and trapped in my state of singleness. Then the Spirit draws my eye to these above texts in Song of Songs and my flesh cringes. "Look away!" it shouts. "That is not meant for you! You have already demonstrated patience. This doesn't apply to someone who has waited as long as you have." My wicked eye looks on this text as a curse and not the boundary, not the provision of God. A struggle ensues between my flesh and my Spirit, for most certainly, "these are in opposition to one another" (**Galatians 5:17**). Now, from experience I know my Spirit will ultimately prevail, but not before my flesh has stabbed at me and handed me over to pride and impatience; not before I have run headlong to awaken a love not pleased by my having woken it, and not before my heart is wounded at best, or crushed at worst. I said a moment ago these verses are the provision of God, and so they are; they are there to be a sentry for our heart. Recently I, with callous disregard, cast these verses aside. After what seemed to be an extremely long four and a half years without looking with affection upon a woman or having spoken tenderly to the fairer sex, I met someone. She was beautiful, intelligent, and loved God and His word. So I pulled myself up out of dating retirement and pursued. But she was honest and forthright and said from the very beginning, "I am not ready." Not to be deterred by her state-ment (which really translated "I am not ready to be aroused or awoken"), I pursued with more vigor. And her heart was won. (For a moment maybe, but never fully.) I enjoyed her and, I believe, she enjoyed me, but her words continued to fall on deaf ears. "Not yet." "I'm just not ready." So having not really heard her, I persisted in my pursuit. Resentment built in her heart and just a few short weeks after it started, it ended. It was devastating for I had set free my heart to love; I had awoken my heart and said "run to love." Her heart was not as affected, as she had never been able to give her heart. But as I said, she was honest and forthright from the very beginning when she said "I am not ready." What's really sad is that I sought counsel from one of my wisest and most trusted advisors before I even pursued this woman. I told my counselor, "She says she isn't ready." My counselor told me, "Just be her friend, but nothing else for now." I can't believe how deaf I was. The Bible screams, "do not arouse or awaken love until she pleases," the girl had said "I'm not ready," and my counselor had said "just friends for now." But impatience had already taken hold of me. Pride said I deserved to be loved and this woman was the one who would love me and nurture me, plus I enjoyed her company and conversation so much. How could I be wrong? I was wrong because love was not ready to be awoken in her. I was wrong because I was not patient. I was wrong because I disregarded too many things. I was just wrong. I wish I could say there are no consequences, but that would be foolishness. I have not been able to retain this young woman as a friend. Had I just started there, today we could be friends who encourage and admonish one another in the Lord, for certainly she knows Him well. Then, of course, there is the bitter sting of loss that had me weeping before God for several weeks. There is the memory of her that should not be mine and with that memory comes pain; not because our time together was bitter, but because it was sweet. It was a gentle reprieve in a routine life. Some would say, and have said, "It is better to have loved and lost than to have never loved at all." I think those people are wrong, unless they are speaking of the death of a spouse, for the best thing would have been to "not arouse or awaken love until she pleases." Be cautious, O single friend. If love is sleeping soundly and seems it would not be stirred, pass by and wait for another time.

CHAPTER TWENTY

THE NEXT TO LAST CHAPTER: if you can call it that

I KNOW I CAN

Everything discussed in these pages in regard to love is possible! You cannot, but God can! Let me leave you with one final thought. When you are less than patient or unkind, when in any way you do not follow the guidelines written out for us in the Bible, you have failed to be a vessel of God's unfailing love. At the exact moment I become impatient with someone, it is at that moment I have ceased to be a vessel of God's perfect love. God never stops loving someone unswervingly. In Christ, you should always say, "I know I can." His love knows no sleep, and His love is the only one there has ever been. So press on to know Him and in your knowing of Him and as you experience His love for you, become a lover of those around you.

THANKS

Thank you for taking the time to read these notes. My prayer is that you would not see me, but would have a better understanding of the Love God has for you and for others. God desires to use you to demonstrate his perfect unfailing love to everyone you come into contact with. I pray God would bless others through you and, in turn, you would be blessed. If you have any further questions or comments or if you would like to have these notes taught to your youth, college, or adult group please feel free to contact me through my website: www.higherrock.org

Since January 1998 I have taught these notes many times for couple's retreats, valentine's banquets, college events, and true love waits seminars. You are also welcome to teach these to the various groups in your church by contacting me for the LOVE NOTES YOUTH CURRICULUM, LOVE NOTES COLLEGE CURRICULUM, or LOVE NOTES ADULT CURRICULUM. I pray that these pages have been both and encouragement and challenge to you.

May God continue to teach you!

Still Learning to Desire God,
ryan

CHAPTER TWENTY-ONE

SHORT STORIES ARE ALWAYS NICE

9-22-04

This is a short story I wrote in 1997-1998, and have always wanted to have it as part of my Love Notes… so I guess it's time. I hope you enjoy this story and that it is able to encourage you in some way. Almost everything means something, so read it carefully. Some is obvious; some is subtle. Enjoy! I'd like to thank my friend Scott for encouraging me to continue the writing of this story when I had planned on throwing it away. Even when I had put it off for seven months it was Scott who pushed me forward. Thanks, brother.

ryan

A MAY EPIC

He was born alone
But was not to live alone
Still, it is not why he was born, nor where
That matters. Nor does it matter what has happened
Between there and here-
For here is where we are and where our concern does
lie

*   *   *   *   *

Calrew:

Calrew kept his bed company long into the morning. It's not that he had nothing to do, but those things did not carry the weight they once had…

"My heart is heavy; laden with weights that all the scales in this prison could not begin a measure of. Oft' I have thought madness was upon me in the midnight's hour, and as I stole a breath of sleep from demons that do taunt me wake, madness himself would creep upon me and bind me with chains and lead balls. It is this very notion that kept me from sleep, along with creatures who dance with scaly feet and iron talons in my brain. But fatigue—that wretched being—was bought by madness to close my eyes, and ever a faithful devil does force me into nightmarish dreams. But whoa, what beast is this outside my chamber window!? A mere spider, truly not. Me thinks sometimes I hear him cry out my name, that spider born of a witch to curse my house and me. He dances in circles to spin a web and does ever more move toward a center point. I myself am danced around in circles. Another's marionette, I do dance on the end of his web and do act a play that I wish no more to be an actor in than I have the power to deny him use of my limbs.

'Calrew.'

The spider called in a voice so faint I am still uncertain as to whether or not it was my name he had called.

'Tis' not madness, boy, that curses you.' Of course, I drew a sharp breath at this, not madness, then who? I shall study this matter further that I might find safety rather than awkward abuse tonight."

*   *   *   *   *

She was born alone
But was not to live alone....

*   *   *   *   *

Watcher:

Evolym is beautiful, and for now we can only be watchers at her window and hear what words those precious lips utter. I see her now; she seems almost lost in pain. Me thinks her eyes do speak of things that Calrew's mind has previously revealed. But that is just a watcher's guess. Listen she speaks.

Evolym:

"Tragic, beautiful, storybook pages. Rivers and birds and wind all sing or howl. They hurt me. But this hurt: this agony; this pain; so warm, my heart is ignited. It gives me a fire. A fire for that which I have never known and therein lies the pain."

Calrew:

"Alas, this study by the oil of midnight has revealed to me an answer. 'Tis not madness, as I once thought. Yet this answer is more a puzzle than that question before. It seems in books and fairy tales and from the pen twixt the fingers of many a man, that there is a villain and a hero with the same face. He is called love. I have ne'er heard such a name uttered before and herein lies the puzzle. Madness I have seen and I'd spy his visage if 'twere lost among a thousand. But love is like a secret murderer whose arrow flies from a secret place to pierce my heart, and yet 'tis not that I have been pierced that hurts my body so. Rather, it is that I have an enemy that stalks me, and I've not seen his form. Yet it is this love that calls me, and here within my heart is a flame to know him. To embrace him and have him fill my bosom. Look now as the sun does rise. It burns forth brightly and its warmth comes from outside similar to a painful fire within."

Watcher:

We are in her bedchamber. I have been careful not to wake this fair Evolym. Her bolted door of wood and iron will not keep us from being watchers. A window shut in stone, it will not keep us out. A walk around her bed. Her silken hair envelops her face. She is beautiful. I have lain next to her as a watcher. But she has not felt me any more than she has felt the wind brush across her cheek, or across her lips. Those were my fingers; that was my kiss. I have only watched her these two days past but I wish it had been a lifetime. This morning her cover silhouettes her form and though I cannot see it for certain, I know these curves here are her breasts, this her body, and these her legs. Frail fingers escape the sheets and I have seen them attached to a lovely hand and porcelain arm. We left Calrew waking the sun, and now the sun wakes our fair Evolym. The light on her face gives an individual the idea of an angel. She turns quietly as her eyes focus on the shades of early hours. A sigh escapes her mouth. There is a tear on her cheek, a smile, Mona Lisa-like, on her lips. Though I'd stay here a thousand years, we must not forget Calrew. Farewell, maid Evolym.

I realize now, looking on Calrew, that I have not told you what he looks like. He is a man of good height, but not great proportion. His eyes like a blue sky or pools of water at a river's edge. His hair in brown locks curls about his face. A dark frame on pale skin. Most oft' he wears a smile but as of late…

I wish I could tell you of Evolym's radiance and so I shall, but of details I am not allowed to speak. But hush! Here is a knock on poor Calrew's chamber door.

Calrew:

"Enter. Ah, my friend and brother, Siwel. What has kept you? The sun has been awake two hours now and I myself did not taste last eve's rest. Please sit, I must ask you a question."

Watcher:

I interrupt only to say that Siwel has been Calrew's companion and friend now for the better half of two turns. He is much the same size as Calrew, only he has nicely trimmed locks of gold upon his brow.

Calrew:

"In my study last night, I released madness from the charges I had brought against him. I have found it is a stranger who calls himself love that does leave my chest empty. Know you of him? Speak his secrets in my ear that I can be wary of his deeds."

Siwel:

"Calrew, yes I know of this love. But it is not a villain as you suppose and it does not form itself as a man. Last eve while you perched yourself in the library and o'er looked books of old, I o'er looked my love. While you caressed yellowed pages, I caressed my love's skin, while your lips read words, mine read the lips of my love. On a breeze I feel her, in the river I hear her. In darkness I miss her and in the daylight I know her warm embrace. Love, my friend, hangs on her whisper, in her perfume, in her touch, or even the mere thought of her. And love is only mine enemy in that distance, miles, separate her from my side. But that shall be remedied before spring gives way to summer. Then she will be mine and I hers."

Calrew:

"You speak riddles, Siwel. I do not know or understand these things you speak of."

Siwel:

"You will, my friend, but now I must away from this place, for my love does anticipate my arrival, and I cannot keep myself from her another moment this day."

Calrew:

"Goodbye, my brother, run if you will, but I shall guard against this devil. I'll not be taken as easily as you have been. Now I am alone again. Why does that prick me so? I have been alone many times. Why then these tears? It is not the absence of Siwel, but those words he spoke; they cause me to bleed. If I were not certain of my breath and beating heart, I would say I'm a corpse. ENOUGH! I WILL TAKE NO MORE ABUSE! I HAVE HAD ENOUGH!

Watcher:

I'm afraid it is an angry scene before us now. Calrew hurt, alone, and angry, grips his clothing and beats his chest. Had not madness been acquitted, I'd swear it was madness himself that gripped Calrew and sent him running down the corridor and out to the stables. But as Calrew races out to the woods on horseback, we know who is to blame. From deep within himself he screams out...

Calrew:

"Love arm yourself, for today I will find you. Today you will fall by my hand or I by yours!"

Evolym:

"The sun this morning does seem to wake a new dawn. It warms me, refreshes me. A kiss soft on my body is the sun in my skin. It renews in me a longing and emptiness, a desire to find that which I have never known. Listen, the birds of the forest do beckon me. It is my name they call from treetops. They are calling me and I'll wait no more!"

Watcher:

Evolym is graceful as she moves. She too has a horse that waits her, and she withdraws from the courtyard to the tender shadows of the woods. Far above, I am like an observer of a beautifully written play. Perchance that is what I am and what I am beholding. For from here, I see Calrew coming this way, and from here, I see Evolym going that way. They are like the two tips of a straight line; when followed they shall meet in the middle, and lest I miss my guess or the two below their way, 'tis only moments and a moment more a'for the meeting twixt the two.

Calrew:

"Love, show yourself! Lest I call you a coward! This is not your home. I have been here since a child and I will not have you disrupt me now! Onward, beast, do not be afraid of the shadows, it is me they want."

Evolym:

"What magic is this, or which tale, riddle, have I fallen into? I now find myself a way that I have ne'er found before, and me here since my childhood. My body feels as though lightning is coursing through it. I do not know why."

Watcher:

Though both Calrew and Evolym have been upon the same earth since their births, their meeting has been delayed for what I expect to be a passionate encounter. Look, here is Calrew coming through the underbrush. He is stopping to water himself and his horse, Patience, at the river's edge.

Calrew:

"Stop here for a moment, Patience, you have been faithful to me, now drink your fill. I too shall cup the cool waters to my lips. Ah, it is cold, but wretched curse that is upon me, I still am thirsty. This grand adventure, this terrible quest to find love and slay him has left me parched beyond what these waters can satisfy."

Evolym:

"Be still, Time, I hear a river running, and there you will find rest from our journey. I will take a moment with you to cool myself there."

Calrew:

"Curse upon you, love, who have struck the water so that I know not contentment. But quiet, what is this I see? My eyes do deceive me, a rider on a white steed in and out of trees. It is none but our enemy Love. I shall conceal myself behind the trees until love does approach the river's edge. Then he will cross to me or I to him. He moves as though he is part of the shadows. I should rather reveal myself and if he be my tormentor he will surely come near me to mock me. Steady, Patience, we shall meet love soon."

Watcher:

"The rider Calrew has just observed, of course, is our dear Evolym and not the enemy he has anticipated. She, on Time, has reached the river's edge. Calrew with Patience watch from the opposing shore and just upriver from the lovely maid. Calrew gasps and his face contorts, for this is not what he suspected it to be. Evolym has just slid from Time and has approached the water. She had let her hair down, and apart from her horse, her gown and form are made evident. She is radiant in the midday light and Calrew has forgotten himself.

Calrew:

"Patience, look at her. She is lovely from afar. Watch as she drinks. It is as though I can see more exact than the hawk. Her lips are rubies that part gently. They drink the water so that they glisten. She is wonderful, but dare I call to her? Patience, she prepares to ride.

Watcher:

In fact, this is true, Evolym and Time now quite refreshed, ride slowly down-river in search of a suitable place to cross. Meanwhile, Calrew leads Patience by the bit and keeps a close eye on this beautiful creature from the river's other side. Still, he has no idea she has in mind to cross over. But now in the excitement, I have forgotten myself and have pushed too far ahead. Let us return to Evolym drinking at the river.

Evolym:

"Time, what is this I see in the shadows!? A man! I think he has spied us. I think I should like to meet him. Let us search for a suitable place to cross and make a friend of this stranger."

Watcher:

Evolym, riding Time, and Calrew, leading Patience, both head down river. But neither party having come this way before knows the only place to cross the river is at the pool of temyeht. (Pronounced tim-yet) At this narrow place in the river, mostly hidden by trees, everything seems to stop for a moment and the river's mighty waters settle. But as I said, it is but a small pool and is often hard to find amongst the overgrowth. Few have ever found it before. But look, both Evolym and Calrew draw near to the pool. Evolym, still on Time, notes the pool and urges Time forward, but Calrew, having lost sight of Evolym and leading Patience, pushes past.

Calrew:

"Blast it, Patience, I saw her, then the trees got so thick I could not, and now, on the other side of the thick growth I look and she is gone! Come, my trusting friend, let me on thy back once more and we shall see if there is not a place we might cross this river."

Watcher:

Meanwhile, Evolym and Time are in the pool; Time enjoying a drink of the sweet waters and Evolym resting on a grassy log that sits like a throne in the midst. Calrew, now on Patience again, has doubled back and from his new perspective notices a narrow opening in the thick trees where he had previously lost sight of Evolym. It is toward this opening that he now moves.

Now it happens in an instant: Calrew rides into the clearing and practically right on top of Evolym. Their eyes meet like flint on flint.

'Hello'

'Hello'

Both are standing in temyeht. The two spend what seems mere minutes in excited talk, but minutes, when shared in the pool of temyeht, turn themselves to months.

In these unknown months, I have seen much. Though I do not understand everything, I will tell that which I've seen. They talk continuously; they want to know more and more about the other. At first, that is all it was, but now it is as if the two are sharing one thought. He finishes her words and she his. I must tell you about the touching. This is too wonderful for my hand to grasp, but I will tell what I have witnessed here. It was not long after Calrew sat down that his hand incidentally, and possibly unintentionally, touched hers; but in that moment she flushed and he caught his breath. She looked at his hand that he had now raised palm toward her. Evolym placed her delicate hand next to his, their fingertips a mere thread of a summer breeze apart and it sent a shudder through their bodies. They moved their fingers slowly back and forth and why she closed her eyes when she smiled, I do not know. But soon their hands were locked. It was not long before he pressed her to himself. Calrew seemed pleased to smell her hair and neck and to brush her cheek with his mouth. This seemed to be right to Evolym as well; she kissed him on the cheek, and he turned his head and kissed her full on the mouth. Amid all this, they shared tales, and tears, and laughter, and more kissing. Then came a time that, I believe, they knew would come. He asked her and she responded favorably. A date was set upon and each went their own way to put their houses in order; they would meet again soon enough. But let us join Calrew and Patience as they put distance between themselves and the river separate.

Calrew:

"Ah, Patience, alas I know love is no villain, but a friend to him he slays! The birds are light in the air today as if the breeze himself carries them away. Their song is new I do believe. But such sweet music must have words. I shall pen a verse for Evolym:

Evolym
My love
A vision at a waters edge
Did draw me nigh to thee
Your voice sang heaven's tunes
Afore it was given to you
Your hand in mine
The most perfect fit
Until your body
Graced mine in hot embrace
And your mouth does drip honey
For your kiss was sweet
And warmed by the sun
Your breath was golden on my cheek
Talk to me Evolym
I long to hear your voice
And I will come
Ne'er to part from your side again

There, a song as sung by me, what think you, Patience? But lo, here is our home and I see Siwel waving us in. Hello dear, Siwel my brother, it seems but a breath since I saw you this morn."

Siwel:

"Calrew 'twas not this morning, but a morning seven months lost. I feared you were lost in the woods of Searching unknowing. I was told you had gone that way when e'er I left. Your house is not yours any longer. I was here just now to see if any news of you was heard and here you are with Patience fresh from the trees."

Calrew:

"Siwel, what do you mean the house is no longer mine? 'Twas mine when I left whether this morning or months gone by, so why not mine now?"

Siwel:

"Calrew, it is as though you never knew its halls, I found my own house this way just two weeks past. My bed was not therein, nor was my name upon the door. It has been the same for my love, my heart, my Devoleb Evod. She found her house in the same manner at the hour I found mine. She knocked on the door and no one there knew her name. Alas, we are staying at a cottage; the innkeeper took us in. He calls the place, The Engagement. He is a cheerful old man with a smile on his lips. They call him, Willu Emyrram. Come friend, Wisdom is saddled and ready; do not dismount Patience yet, but follow me to The Engagement."

Watcher:

So this is what happens. Calrew has found his house no longer his, yet strangely feels no loss and is following his friend Siwel and Siwel's beast Wisdom to the Inn Engagement where a smiling innkeeper and the lovely Devoleb Evod wait. Meanwhile, Evolym has returned home to find there is none and is staying with a friend.

Evolym:

"I shan't be here long. But two days and one and I shall meet Calrew again. Then we will be joined. Between here and there days will pass like years, and the nights will be a sleepless prison. But on three mornings hence, I will start alive and with Time will meet my love.

Watcher:

The days did pass slowly. The first morning took years to grow into nightfall. The second morning called darkness a stranger and the second night wickedly taunted Calrew awake; for he knew on the morrow he would seek out his Evolym and to her he would be joined.

Calrew:

"What a weight upon my chest that keeps me from drawing a full breath. And my heart does thunder vehemently within my bosom. I think I'd so be filled with joy at the waking of the morn that my heart might tire itself out with this incessant beating. My mind does make me crazy at my longing for the fairest Evolym. But alas! The Dawn! Awake, Patience, and let us seek out Evolym.

Watcher:

Calrew leaves his friend Siwel sleeping, and rides softly out of the yard. But at a distance fair enough so that no sleeping soul may be woken, Calrew spurs Patience on to a gallop.

Evolym:

"It is a quiet morning! This day has found me though for a time I was certain it had misplaced itself. I cannot be bound any further. I will run to Calrew and today he will be mine and I shall be his. We will be joined that none may separate us.

Watcher:

Calrew was on his way as was Evolym to the Golden Rings. This is the place where all come to be joined. Simply, it is a group of cedars all in a circle; they stand high as clouds and wide as three horses abreast each other. They shine gold by day and night. They are brilliant! I know already in your mind you are picturing them, but perhaps you would like to know this great circle is made up of sixty powerful cedars. I have never seen them grow taller, nor have I ever seen them laid down. They have just always been. Yet, I am not finished telling of this fine meeting place. Just inside this grand golden ring there is another, this one slightly smaller than the cedars and made of eighty firs. These eighty shine in the same bright gold as the cedars. Inside these two rings, there is the feeling of strength unknown to those outside. Still, this is not all the beauty of the place. In the very center of these mighty trees is a single lily. A flower so fair and lovely the trees of gold might as well have been thorns. All of this is a mystery to me, but this place is where the lover and the loved are joined.

Here is where Calrew and Evolym would meet. But enough now of the Golden Rings, here comes Calrew through the Woods of Darkness. But forgive me, my friend, for once again I have leapt forward and forgotten myself. After Calrew left Engagement, he headed toward Higher Rock. Higher Rock is a mountain and it is said that only from the height of Higher Rock can one see the cedars and firs of Golden Rings standing above the other forest trees. Only from that place can one know the direction they are to go. It does not take much time for one to find the height of Higher Rock, in fact, if you stay on the path of Praying Seeking, as Calrew tried to do, you should be on the heights in a moment. Let us join Calrew as he reaches the Heights.

Calrew:

"Patience, look at this! Never have I seen such a beautiful place. The air here is sweet and I feel fresh to breathe it. Look! It is the Golden Rings! From here they pierce the clouds. We have found them, Patience! Let us move ever forward to Evolym; I can stand this separation from her no longer."

Watcher:

It is after this mountain top experience that Calrew, with Patience, began his descent. Only neither of them knew what perils await them in darkness. It only took a moment on the downward slope for a fog putrid as sulfur to engulf them. It is called the forgetting fog. The fog caused Calrew discomfort and Patience was uneasy, and before anything could

226

be done to keep it from being so, the two were lost in darkness. So thick was the darkness and so powerful was forgetting that the two were brought to a standstill. Finally a decision was made, a direction picked, and after hours of pointless wandering, another direction taken. Where was he going and why could he not find it? Calrew and Patience, weary from being lost in darkness, began to search for place enough where the two of them could rest. Up until now, Calrew had not noticed the trees were so close together not even a dwarf had room to sleep.

Calrew:

"Soft, Patience, a brook! Oh, how I thirst for a drink to wet my tongue! This darkness saps me dry!"

Watcher:

It is true they heard a brook, but it was best if they had not. Still, they found it and drank from it. Oh, that I had never seen it come to this; that I could have stopped them. Its waters taste so sweet, but the mind, the heart, do suffer worse than the lips. A heart and mind so affected by the forest darkness and forgetting fog, stand almost no chance when combined with the bitter brook. The three together, and a man has lost himself. Still they drank and moved on. The darkness sets in as hopelessness, and the forgetting fog does so rot the brain that the view of Higher Rock and the path of Praying Seeking are left behind. The bitter brook, as I have said, combined with the other two most often finds a man a grave and buries him without remorse. It was obvious it only took a moment for the waters to take effect. Calrew became uneasy in the saddle and Patience uneasy with his bridle. Both were uneasy with the company of the other. Calrew blamed Patience for the darkness and the fog. Patience was suddenly much too slow for Calrew and was no longer pleasing to him. No sooner has Calrew screamed at the blackness and cursed Patience than did a chill cut so quickly through him that his voice was lost and his hair rose ominously on his neck. Patience had flinched at the chill, and had we seen his eyes, we'd have found the terror brought by death. A low rumble was heard like approaching thunder. Calrew leapt from Patience but held tightly to the reins. The thunder echoed until Calrew was certain an army was upon him. As suddenly as it had started and surrounded him, it stopped. The thunder was replaced by a myriad of glowing eyes and gleaming fangs, all of which belonged to the foxes of the forest. Calrew had nowhere to go; he knew that and so did the thousand eyes pointed in his direction, so no one moved. Then, as if upon cue, a low growl emanated from twixt each set of silver teeth and Calrew threw his hands about his ears and fell to the ground; it was by this sign the foxes knew it was their turn to move. In a frenzy that Calrew wished he'd never seen, the foxes were upon Patience. Patience had only a moment of terror in his eyes until he was no more. And with that, the murderous henchmen were gone. Calrew was left terrified, staring over at a pile of clean bones. Patience was as though he never had been. I hated to watch this and hated to see Calrew frozen for hours, unable to speak. When finally Calrew's mind came back to him, though not completely, he thought to make a fire. At this too, I wish I could have spoken out. In the forest darkness, you can build a fire, and it can blaze furiously, but the darkness is so strong that neither light nor heat can be perceived. Calrew, in fact, was successful in building a fire, but never knew it and found himself again cursing the sky that began or ended somewhere above him in the unperceivable tops of invisible trees.

Calrew:
    "CURSE THE DARKNESS!!"

Watcher:
    It was an uneasy sleep he found that night. When he woke, though he was not awake—it was actually a dream—he walked himself to the edge of the forest darkness. It was there he found the army he had earlier feared, a great army, all twice the size of any man he had ever seen, all riding horses three times as high as the tallest horse he'd ever found. Each soldier wore an elaborately decorated breast piece. The picture found there was of a woman bound securely standing among the bones of a horse. Calrew became frantic and looked to and fro, until his eyes rested upon fair Evolym bound and standing just beneath these giants among a pile of bones. With an evil snare, one soldier thrust his lance through the bosom of Evolym and she fell softly with only a whimper. Calrew screamed a cry of terror; it was the

echo of this shout that pulled him from his sleep. As we know, he had never reached the edge of the forest and had not witnessed the death of Evolym. Still, in that place between sleep and wake, he was not yet sure what had happened. Then as the reality of the darkness set in, he began to weep. It was here that he knew he would never see Evolym. As he wept, words failed to come forth from his lips. It was at this point of wordlessness that Calrew started at a noise just behind him. He did not care if it was the foxes come to devour him, or if it were some other monstrous beast. However, it was neither fox nor beast. Calrew turned to gaze upon…light! Light in the forest darkness! Calrew was shocked, but I had seen this light before. This blinding sun in the middle of this blackness emanated from a bird lovely in form, with fire upon its breast and wings. This giant blazing bird lit on a branch near the head of Calrew.

"Do not be afraid." It spoke softly. "I am here to be your tongue, your voice. My name is Tirips." Calrew had heard of Tirips before and even believed he existed, but to see him was a sight amazing.

"Why do you despair?" Tirips asked. "Why did you fail to keep Patience? Why do you act as though there is no hope? You have forgotten DROL!"

Calrew:

"I know of DROL, oh mighty Tirips. I have heard of Him and have even called Him Rehtaf."

Watcher:

Calrew did in fact know of DROL. DROL was the keeper of all things and guardian and maker of all life. He was known as the Protector, and to some The Sword and The Shield. To others, He was known as a great healer; to others, a Savior of the dying. Calrew had called Him Rehtaf, which was a sign, a word of great affection; a term deeming Calrew as part of DROL'S family.

Calrew:

"Do not speak to me of DROL who is the sun, and the sword, and the shield! Do not speak of Him as a healer! Do not tell me He is Rehtaf! If He were a sword, He would have destroyed those devouring foxes; if a healer, He would have restored Patience to life; if Rehtaf, He would have kept me from this darkness!"

Watcher:

It was with this that Tirips blazed so brightly Calrew thought for sure He would consume Himself. Suddenly, this timid bird became a booming Phoenix.

"WHO IS THIS THAT DARKENS MY COUNSEL WITH WORDS WITHOUT KNOWLEDGE? BRACE YOURSELF LIKE A MAN; I WILL QUESTION YOU, AND YOU SHALL ANSWER ME. WHERE WERE YOU WHEN I LAID THE EARTH'S FOUNDATION? HAVE YOU EVER GIVEN ODERS TO THE MORNING; OR SHOWN THE DAWN ITS PLACE, THAT IT MIGHT TAKE

THE EARTH BY ITS EDGES? DO YOU SEND THE LIGHTNING BOLTS ON THEIR WAY? DO THEY REPORT TO YOU, 'HERE WE ARE'? WOULD YOU DISCREDIT MY JUSTICE? WOULD YOU CONDEMN ME TO JUSTIFY YOURSELF? FOLLOW ME, YOU MAN MADE OF THE DUST OF THE GROUND. TAKE HOLD OF MY FIREY TAIL AND WE WILL FIND DROL AND YOU CAN TAKE YOUR ARGUMENT BEFORE HIM."

Calrew obeyed Tirips and, oddly enough, the fire did not burn his flesh. Tirips moved rapidly twixt the trees and came to a stop in an opening only big enough for Calrew to stand.

"What is it you see here, Calrew?" Tirips asked.

"I see an almond tree." Calrew replied.

"You are right for saying this!" Tirips landed atop the almond tree and communicated with it in a language Calrew had never heard. After only a moment, Tirips returned to Calrew.

"DROL is watching you and will watch you from here."

I believe Calrew must have been overcome with conviction because he threw his hands into the dark air and wept out loud. His tears mixed with words that struggled from his throat. I could not understand him more than he was sorry for forgetting DROL and for cursing Him. His words, however, must have been both heard and pleasing to Tirips, because Tirips fell so completely on Calrew, for a moment he was lost from my sight. Then a voice boomed, not from Tirips, but rather from the almond tree. I knew it to be the voice of DROL, and Calrew must have known it too because he fell suddenly quiet.

"CALREW, I HAVE WATCHED YOU! I HAVE HEARD YOU! I AM HE THAT YOU HAVE CALLED REHTAF. I AM STILL HIM AND I SHALL EVER BE. YOU ARE MY CHILD, BECAUSE YOU HAVE DIED BUT STILL ARE ALIVE. NOW YOU HAVE BEEN IN FOREST DARKNESS FOR FORTY DAYS, BUT DO NOT FEAR, FOR YOU WILL FIND EVOLYM WAITING FOR YOU. HER JOURNEY HAS ALSO TAKEN UNTIL NOW. I HAVE TESTED YOU AND HAVE KNOWN YOUR ANXIOUS THOUGHTS! BUT TIRIPS HAS SPOKEN FOR YOU AND NOW, LOOK; HERE IS YOUR PRECIOUS PATIENCE. I HAVE RESTORED HIM TO YOU. GO ON IN HIM AND DO NOT FORGET ME!"

With that, the ground shook and Calrew fell facedown; when he looked up, he found a meadow beneath his face, Patience at his side, and the forest darkness at his back. Calrew mounted Patience and found him stronger and lovelier than ever before. The two of them found their strength renewed and ran tirelessly through the meadow as an eagle upon the wind. In no more than a heartbeat of a lover, Calrew and Patience found the golden rings and rode into the midst of them at the moment that Evolym, ever on Time, came from the other direction. These two, one the lover and one the beloved, came together at the center of the rings near the earlier-mentioned lily. Never before had Calrew been more enamored than he was now. The two touched hands softly and left them there for a moment. Calrew kissed her lightly on the lips. Soon, the two lay on a verdant bed of grass and flowers. Behind them, and without their knowledge, sat an almond tree, and a dogwood tree. Tirips came from the sky and rested a wing on each of the two trees. In a flash there was no separation, no distinction between the three. They were one blazing fire. This fire, imposing in stature, moved toward the young couple. These lovers were naked and unashamed. He continued to kiss her mouth. Their kisses were long, wet, and warm. He embraced her, never to let go. Still, the fire came nearer. He was a gazelle on her mountains of spice. He drank the honey from under her tongue. Still ever nearer came the fire. She loved the feel of him. This I knew by her smile and her emanation of affection. She opened her garden to him and he held for the first time its treasures. And the fire was at their backs. Finally, she invited him into her and he came so close to her and seemed to fill her so completely, that it was hard to distinguish where she ended and he began. And the fire was upon them, consuming them. I heard their cries, not of anguish, but of joy. And the fire melted them. As the fire finished its job, it began to move on and it cried out "EAT, O FRIENDS, AND DRINK; DRINK YOUR FILL O LOVERS." When it had moved by them, I saw not Evolym or Calrew, but instead I saw one single life. The voice of DROL rang out:

"YOU ARE NOT NOW CALREW OR EVOLYM, BUT NOW I HAVE CALLED YOUR NAME UNION. PATIENCE AND TIME HAVE

BEEN MADE AS ONE AND I CALL THEM TO MY GLORY. NOW, UNION, RIDE UPON TO MY GLORY AND WHAT I HAVE BROUGHT TOGETHER, LET NO ONE TEAR APART. I WILL BE EVER WITH YOU AND I WILL BE YOUR DROL AND YOU WILL BE MY HANDS AND MY FEET. I HAVE ORDAINED THESE TWO SHOULD BE UNION AND MY WORD IS GOOD AND RIGHT. NOW GO AND FOLLOW THE PATH PRAYING SEEKING, AND BUILD YOUR HOME ON HIGHER ROCK. CALL TO ME AND I WILL ANSWER YOU AND SHOW YOU GREAT AND UNSEARCHABLE THINGS YOU DO NOT KNOW."

So they did just as they were told, and Union, ever with To My Glory, lived on Higher Rock, the home of DROL. They sought Him and obeyed His voice, and the winds and the rains never swept them away and they were never shaken. Thus ends the tale of Calrew and Evolym, and here begins the tale of Union. I, a watcher, have recorded all I have seen and heard and now I write no more.

Printed in the United States
108913LV00001B/145-177/P